DATE DUE

NOV 2 6 2000

THE WAY OF THE
★ WARRIOR ★

BUSINESS TACTICS AND TECHNIQUES FROM

HISTORY'S TWELVE GREATEST GENERALS

THE WAY OF THE
★ WARRIOR ★

BUSINESS TACTICS AND TECHNIQUES FROM

HISTORY'S TWELVE GREATEST GENERALS

JAMES DUNNIGAN AND DANIEL MASTERSON

A·THOMAS·DUNNE·BOOK

ST. MARTIN'S PRESS ★ NEW YORK

A THOMAS DUNNE BOOK.
An imprint of St. Martin's Press.

Library of Congress Cataloging-in-Publication Data

Dunnigan, James F.
    The way of the warrior : leadership lessons from history's top
  twelve great military masters   /   James Dunnigan and Daniel Masterson.
        p.   cm.
    Includes bibliographical references and index.
    ISBN 0-312-17061-0
    1. Management.   2. Leadership.   3. Success in business.
  4. Militarism.   I. Masterson, Daniel M.   II. Title.
  HD31.D843   1997
  658—dc21   97-20324
                                                                    CIP

Design by Junie Lee

First Edition: November 1997

10   9   8   7   6   5   4   3   2   1

To the rest of the Mastersons: Darla, Chersti, Travis, Westen, and Daniel for their love, support, and patience.

Acknowledgments

A number of people with military and management experience read the manuscript and contributed many valuable comments and criticisms. Thus, we would like to thank Stephen B. Patrick, Bill Speer, Al Nofi, Mike Macedonia, Trent Telenko, Fun Fong, Kurt Aldag, Shaun Coyne, Tim Keenon, Neal Bascomb, Scott Rosenthal, Karen Little, and Mike Ley.

CONTENTS

THE WAY OF THE
★WARRIOR★

BUSINESS TACTICS AND TECHNIQUES FROM

HISTORY'S TWELVE GREATEST GENERALS

CHAPTER I

WARRIORS AND MANAGEMENT

GREAT GENERALS AND successul managers have a lot in common. Don't be misled by the battles and fancy uniforms. The warriors of legend, the commanders who achieved dramatic feats on the battlefield, were, first and foremost, highly effective managers. Think about it. During a military career, a general might fight only a few, to a few dozen, battles. Most fight none at all. Campaigns would consume more time, often months or years of just moving troops around and, more importantly, keeping them fed, clothed, equipped, and ready for combat. But campaigns don't always result in many, or any, actual battles. The skills required to manage a campaign successfully were those that separated "Great Captains" from the rest of the pack. Thus most of a Great Captain's time was spent managing. Before, or in between wars, it was all management. During wars it was still mostly dealing with a mountain of detail and nonlethal decision making. Generals who were poor managers often had their armies fall apart before battle was joined, or else quickly collapse under the stress of combat.

In war, it is preparation that makes the difference. If the troops reach the battlefield hungry, poorly trained, and with shabby equipment and weapons, they will not do very well. Indeed, they will probably lose. Actually, there have been so few competent generals through the centuries that the saying, "it's not a matter of who's better, but who's worse" came into use. This quip recognized the fact that both sides in most battles were usually badly led, and victory often went to the side least unready for combat. But here we shall examine the cream of the crop, the Great Captains who so outclassed their competition, they usually rolled over a long string of opponents, restrained only by mortality or going one conquest too far.

While much is made of tactical skill when commanding troops in combat, even this is a talent developed from many years of practice and painstaking preparation. Training troops for battle is another of those management skills Great Captains possess, the ability to inspire their soldiers to endure months or years of drills, developing an edge that ultimately produces spectacular battlefield results.

In combat, the great military commanders have had to solve multiple problems quickly and often while new crises were developing around them. This ability to get things done while your world is falling down about your ears is a talent most people in business would like to have. The best examples of good management under stress can be obtained from the Great Captains of history. Then again, many highly regarded peacetime commanders have proved failures in the cauldron of combat. That's another lesson from military history. Managing is one thing, managing combined with leading under fire is an altogether different animal, and a rare one to boot. A manager may do quite well when things are calm but then crumple under the pressure when the situation gets more, well, exciting.

Thus while the Great Captains were not businessmen, they did have to worry about managing. Great military commanders are, after all, managers most of the time. Victory in battle is 90 percent preparation and 10 percent taking care of unanticipated emergencies. How did the Great Captains do this? Our research indicates they did it using ancient, and still viable, management techniques. What we are doing in this book is spotlighting the techniques used by the Great Captains and pointing out how their use of these techniques provides useful lessons for today's managers.

Until this century, "management" was not discussed as a discipline. The ancients would sometimes speak of statecraft and tips on how to manage a farm. But for those rare few with a natural talent for managing large organizations, it was largely a process of reinventing the wheel each time a major military crisis brought into existence those large organizations known as armies. Until the past century or so, there was nothing like the large modern business to manage, except armies.

It is amazing to see how each of the Great Captains of the past used the same, or very similar, techniques to organize their way to victory. We have gathered together this ancient wisdom and present it in terms modern business people can understand.

But the Great Captains also show us how to deal with what affects current businesspeople at every level—information overload. The Great Captains stood at the top of large pyramids of power. Masses of information, much of it fragmentary and suspect, washed over them. They had to come up with ways to deal with this in the days before telephones, CNN, and satellite communications. One of the greatest problems managers then, and now, have had to deal with is handling the masses of information coming in during times of stress. The ancients figured out how to handle it, as well as how to take care of time and space problems that still exist in our age of instant communication.

WAY OF THE WARRIOR WOMEN

Where are the female Great Captains? Simple, there aren't any. Women have been active in military affairs throughout the centuries, but not as universally or enthusiastically as the men. Part of the reason for this is tradition, but that in turn is based on more practical considerations.

Before muskets and rifles came into wide use during the last few centuries, combat was mostly about brute strength. The weapons, such as swords and spears, were wielded by hand. Bows required up to a hundred pounds of pull. Armor required strength to carry. A leader of warriors had to be more than a leader: he had to be someone the troops would respect as one of their own. Given that situation, there were far fewer opportunities for a military-minded female to get started on a military career, especially a career as spectacular as those studied here.

Not that female military leaders were absent. There were many, largely the able members of powerful families. Often, in times of crises, these women would step into a power vacuum and take charge of the troops.

Women have always been more prominent as national leaders, for that job does not require an apprenticeship in arms. Thus in the seventh century, as the victorious Arab Moslem armies swept across North

Africa, they were brought up short by a Berber army led by a woman, the Kahena Dahiyan of Barbary. She was the leader of one of the Jewish tribes in the region, and she forged an alliance with the other nomadic tribes and settled peoples in order to resist the Arabs. She also led the army when need be and held off the Arabs for a decade. Her military skills led to several notable victories. But by the early eighth century, an endless supply of Arab troops and Arab money for bribes destroyed her coalition and her resistance.

During the medieval period, female nobles were commonly in charge of castles and entire regions and kingdoms while their husbands were away campaigning. Again, this defense of fortified areas relied largely on brains and leadership, not brute strength and the ability to physically impress a bunch of muscular warriors on a battlefield. During a siege, everyone could help out on the walls, either throwing things at the attacking troops or making emergency repairs. The notable female leaders of this period only rarely had to lead in combat. Most of their best work was done in peacetime. Getting a castle ready for combat was more critical than bold leadership during a siege. If the castle wasn't ready for a fight, leadership alone wouldn't save it.

Today, with most armies comprised largely of people in uniform who do not handle weapons but provide essential support services, more women are able to gain experience in leading troops. The combat jobs still rely on a lot of muscle and other male characteristics. But these "warrior" jobs comprise as little as 15 percent of the troops in many armies. Eventually, the "muscle" jobs will be an even smaller portion of the armed forces. Meanwhile, robots take on more and more battlefield jobs, leaving the military leadership posts available to anyone with the brains, and desire, to excel in combat. At some point, we'll see how important male aggressiveness and relative enthusiasm for combat will affect the percentage of Great Captains that are women.

MANAGEMENT STYLES THROUGH THE AGES

Our Great Captains are a varied lot, spanning twenty-four hundred years of history. The worlds they lived in differed from our own in many important details. Most of the earlier Great Captains were also kings and had to manage nations as well as lead armies. This is not as different from the present as it might appear. Ancient kings were often absolute rulers in name only. As today, the powers of the head of state were often more theoretical than practical. A kingdom was first established when an exceptional individual assembled it out of many pieces, using his wits and skill on the battlefield. The family, in the person of subsequent heirs, tried to keep the kingdom together. Since the sons are rarely identical to their fathers, keeping the crown usually proved to be more of a challenge than establishing it in the first place. Those of our Great Captains who were kings inherited their crowns and had to scramble and improvise to hang on to what Daddy left them. A king inheriting his position had to be quick to size up what the situation was. This was often more of a challenge than it appeared because the new king was often an inexperienced fellow in his twenties or younger. Dad's associates were generally older and more adept in the ways of royal politics. More to the point, these older fellows often had different objectives. Some wanted more independence from the crown, others wanted the crown itself. Assassination and rebellion were common, and a Great Captain wanna-be's first conquest often had to be his own kingdom. Power has always been a lightning rod that attracted unpleasant surprises for those who would be top dog.

Yet these kings were in situations very similar to a new CEO of a large corporation. While assassination or pitched battles are not usually faced by senior management in the twentieth century, there is the same tangle of existing relationships, rivals, and potential allies to be sorted out before the new boss can take control and move the enterprise forward. Don't be misled by all the fancy communications gear and high-tech executive toys. The key management tool is still words, delivered face-to-face. Hasn't changed since the dawn of time and is not likely to in the future.

Our Great Captains also vary considerably in their cultural backgrounds. Anyone who has dealt with foreigners on commercial matters knows that cultural differences can be formidable. Yet those customs are also easily mastered, as these conventions are just different rules of the same game. All of the Great Captains we cover used, for example, parties to schmooze with friends, enemies, and potential allies alike. Entertainment customs varied, and still do, but the basic drill is the same. German, Japanese, American, and British executives all go out drinking. They do this as a means of breaking the ice and getting to know one another better. They do it a bit differently, but sitting around a table and getting drunk can have only so many variations. This is an old routine. Alexander the Great did this; some said he did it to excess. But who's going to argue with a king? U. S. Grant was also criticized for hitting the sauce too often. When someone complained to President Lincoln about Grant's drinking habits, Old Abe was said to have asked if a barrel of whatever Grant was drinking could be sent to each of the other Union generals. Thus while the Great Captains differed in language and customs, they all faced the same problems and had to develop remarkably similar solutions.

As one would expect, our Great Captains were a macho bunch. That's part of the military style and has been around for thousands of years. Even here, there is considerable variation. Some Great Captains, personified in-your-face military macho. Others, like U. S. Grant, were low-key to the point of invisibility (he often wore a common soldier's uniform without insignia). Modern commercial enterprises also tend to be led by aggressive males (and, increasingly, females). While many people in armies, and businesses, can be low-key types, the people leading the operation, the Great Captains, have to be on the ball and on the go. Thus the aggression and the macho. Don't be misled by some low-key CEO. When the situation calls for decisiveness, said CEO is either going to kick out the jams and get the problem solved, or quickly become an ex-CEO. Here we will discuss the people who get things done, not those who shrink from a challenge.

BUSINESS BEFORE BATTLES

As we point out again and again here, military success springs from a lot of nonmilitary activities. Troops must be recruited, equipped, trained, and then maintained for months or years before they see battle. All of these chores require nonmilitary skills. Even training troops is largely a matter of organization. This might seem odd, but look a little closer and you'll see the nonmilitary underpinnings of combat training. Military training involved learning two different types of skills, both of which have always had nonmilitary counterparts. Individual training covered the obvious, such as how to use weapons. Spears, swords, bows, and now rifles have always had nonlethal counterparts. In times past, there were farm implements to be mastered. Either learn how to use them well, or starve. And until the nineteenth century, over 80 percent of the world's population made their living with farm implements. Today, over 80 percent of soldiers rarely touch a rifle, but most do use complex equipment. Again, the gear most troops now use is quite similar to what they deal with as civilians. Thus most basic military training is nearly identical to what can be found outside of uniform. Therefore, an executive who excels at training large numbers of factory workers would probably also do well training lots of soldiers at once. And during the two world wars of this century, civilian managers got to do just that quite a lot, as armies rapidly expanded and skilled civilian executives were put into uniform to do what they had always done so well.

The other aspect of individual training had to do with just living in the rough while on campaign. Soldiers who learned how to get a good night's sleep, eat well, and avoid disease while marching about for weeks on end were superior soldiers. This military camping out has never been a familiar experience for most people. Thus those who were conversant with the vagabond lifestyle, such as nomads, had a considerable military advantage. Most people, throughout history, come from settled areas where roughing it was avoided.

An army on the march suffers tremendous wear and tear even without any combat. Until this century, you could expect to lose half your troops in six months of marching around, and still more if there were any battles. Most would be sick or injured from constant marching, outdoor living, and unsanitary conditions. World War I was the first major war where combat deaths exceeded losses from disease and exposure. Over the centuries there have been cultures that got into the habit of training their troops to live healthy when camping out. The Romans, over two thousand years ago, developed the most effective system for armies living in the field. No one outdid the Romans in this department until this century. Much of the Roman soldiers' training was about how to set up and maintain the camp, which was done at the end of each day's march. This kind of training was not unknown in civilian life, as large farming and construction enterprises required many people to learn how to work together. The Romans were big on large-scale projects and were able to adapt these civilian practices to military use.

The most obvious large-scale military training is lining the troops up in combat formations and practicing marching around as if in combat. This was a uniquely military activity, but, as you can see, only a small part of the training an effective soldier would receive. Through thousands of year and hundreds of cultures, the advantage of better-trained soldiers was demonstrated. In the West, training methods became more effective and widely used over the last few centuries. This training edge was largely an organizational one. Commercial enterprises provided the models for the Great Captains to copy from. This more lethal military system existed in the West several centuries before the rest of the world adopted it. Military commanders in the West had the opportunity to make use of local commercial advances in organization and training and, like soldiers everywhere, they used what was available to enhance their chances on the battlefield.

All of our Great Captains, with the exception of Genghis Khan, are from the West. And Genghis was included partly because of the impact he had on the West. But we have concentrated on Great Captains in the West because they would be more familiar and because the West has been the premier practitioner of war over the last few centuries. Western innovators invented what we know as modern warfare. Western businessmen also invented modern management techniques over the same period, which had a lot to do with Western military success.

There have always been military commanders from other parts of the world, and in the same league with their Western counterparts. But this has been more true in past centuries. In the last hundred years or so, the non-Western Great Captains have largely been practitioners of irregular warfare. Two of the most obvious examples this century have been Mao Zedong of China and Vo Nguyen Giap of Vietnam. Both led what we would call guerilla armies and did quite well against a formidable array of opponents (including U.S. troops in both cases). Yet these Eastern Great Captains used the same basic tools as their Western counterparts. Ironically, in the case of these two Communist generals, they adopted Western management techniques via a Western political movement (Communism) that incorporated many late-model Western organizational and technical practices. The Communists perfected the use of political propaganda, secret police, totalitarian government, and a lot of other unpleasant, but effective, tools. They did it by adopting techniques first developed in the commercial sector. Mao and Giap used their political tools in their military organizations and operations, yet another example of the military borrowing from the civilian world.

The basic techniques of the Great Captains have been the same, no matter what part of the world the commander came from or how long ago he wielded power. Superior organization, training, and discipline are constants throughout history. The consistent success of the same techniques makes the experience of these Great Captains very valuable for the modern manager. Here are management practices that have stood the test of time, culture, and the most severe crises.

Read on and learn what it takes to cope with the ultimate management challenges.

CHAPTER 2

★ ALEXANDER THE GREAT ★

THE BIG, BIG VISION

ALEXANDER THE GREAT, who twenty-four hundred years ago led Greek forces to conquer the much larger Persian Empire, and then some, had the vision of uniting many different cultures over a vast geographic area. Uniting the cultures, rather than just conquering them, was a unique idea at the time. Although his fame springs largely from military conquests, his deliberate political and social policies created a Hellenized civilization from India to Egypt and north to the Caucasus and Afghanistan. Pieces of his empire, still governed by Greeks, survived for centuries after Alexander's death. Alexander's techniques for merging disparate cultures are still viable to this day. As a manager, Alexander thought and acted on a grand scale, a scale no one before him had attempted, much less succeeded at. Alexander operated on a broad palette but also paid attention to details to a degree rarely seen before, or since.

THE WORLD OF ALEXANDER (356–323 B.C.)

Alexander was Macedonian, belonging to an ancient aristocratic family in an area northeast of Greece that, at the time, was not quite Greek. But Alexander himself, born in 356 B.C., the son of King Philip of Macedon, began life a few jumps ahead of your average fourth-century B.C. European. Of medium (under five feet nine inches) height, fair-complexioned, and with an athletic build, Alexander received an excellent education. One of his tutors was the Greek philosopher Aristotle. Alexander developed a lifelong love of learning. The Greek world was one of thought and learning, and Alexander was ahead of the curve in this area also.

Macedonia had been, for centuries, a frontier area between the civilized Greek city-states and the equally advanced Persian and Greek cities to the east in Anatolia (modern day Turkey) and beyond. To the north and west were tribes and more primitive kingdoms, whose peoples spoke many different languages, a situation which contributed to frequent wars. Beyond Macedonia's vague and constantly shifting borders were about a million and a half tribal peoples in what is now the Balkans.

Macedonia itself was only sporadically united. The Greeks considered the Macedonians a bunch of upcountry roughnecks and bumpkins. Most Macedonians cared little for the Greeks, seeing them as effete city slickers. Numbering about five hundred thousand people when Alexander was born, about half the Macedonians lived back in the hills and were organized on a tribal basis. The rest of the population lived on the coastal plain, in and around the larger towns and cities of Macedonia. Back then, any built-up place with walls surrounding it and a population of over ten thousand people was considered a "city."

But the Macedonian merchants and the nobility did care for Greece, and especially Greek culture. This was the golden age of Greek thought and intellectual progress. Moreover, there had been Greek migration into Macedonia for centuries. Most of these Greeks were merchants, artisans, and the children of prominent Greeks marrying into the Macedonian upper class. The top few percent of Macedonians spoke Greek and had their children educated by Greek tutors.

The population as a whole saw themselves as part of the Greek world and, as was common with everyone in the Greek "community," felt they were just a bit superior to everyone else in the group. The Macedonians shared the Greek antipathy for the Persians across the Aegean Sea. But the bad feeling among Greeks toward Persians went deeper.

There were many Greek settlements, including some large cities, in Anatolia ("Asia Minor," modern-day Turkey) and along the Black Sea coast. These colonial Greeks were often controlled by the Persians and generally chafed at being subject to a "foreign" power. Since about

750 B.C. the Greeks had been colonizing the coastal areas of the Mediterranean and Black Seas. They had been a minority in most areas they settled. By Alexander's time, there were some three hundred thousand Greeks in Asia Minor, with over three million non-Greeks in the interior. The Greek cities thrived on trade and good relations with the non-Greeks (Indo-European peoples, many related to modern-day Armenians) of the interior. But for the previous century and a half the region had been controlled by the Persian Empire.

The Persians, from modern-day Iran (and the ancestors of today's Iranians) ruled an empire of twenty million people, but only about 10 percent were Persians. The empire stretched from Pakistan to Asia Minor and south to Egypt. The Persians were a rough bunch and well organized. If you behaved, and paid your taxes, the Persians left you alone. But the taxes were heavy, often over 10 percent of income each year, and most of it had to be paid in cash. While up to half of this money was spent locally, the rest went back to the capital in Persia (Iran), and a goodly amount was stored, as coin, in the royal treasury. At the time of Alexander, this hoard of silver and gold amounted to some five billion dollars (in modern values), some 10 percent of the empire's GDP. The taxes, and withdrawal of coin from circulation, were a burden on the economy and a source of frequent revolts against Persian rule. In addition, there was usually a civil war when a king died, as there was no accepted routine for selecting the next ruler. Various candidates fought, while portions of the empire rebelled. The rebellions were eventually put down, and a goodly portion of the royal treasury was spent to bribe officials and hire mercenaries.

While the ethnic Persian army comprised ten thousand cavalry and up to fifty thousand infantry, these were not sufficient to hold the entire empire together. Moreover, about half the Persian troops were only called up in wartime, as it was politically too dangerous to have many Persian troops sitting around idle, just waiting for the next civil war. Thus mercenaries were used extensively, usually including, in the 300s B.C., ten to twenty thousand from Greece. The Persian king's money was good, and mercenary soldiering was an ancient and respected profession. The Persians typically sent troops from one part of the empire to garrison areas far from home. This prevented the locals and the royal garrison from becoming too chummy.

The Greek colonies in Asia Minor had been conquered by the new Persian Empire in 550 B.C., and had regularly rebelled against their "foreign" rulers. The cities of Greece would often send troops and money to assist the rebels. The Persians knew how to deal with rebellions, and people who assisted rebels. Thus between 499 and 479 B.C. there were two failed Persian invasions of Greece. The energetic efforts of two Persian kings failed to conquer Greece, but the Asia Minor colonies came back under Persian control. Greece itself was saved by its warships and the determination of its outnumbered soldiers. Greece was always a maritime power, and this struggle with the Persians showed them what they could do when they united their forces. The fighting went on (and off) for fifty years, with the Greeks gaining more and more control over bits and pieces of Persian territory.

By 448 B.C., the Persians decided enough was enough, and other arrangements could be negotiated with the Greeks over controlling Asia Minor. The Persians were practical people, and a few generations after the two invasions, peace was made and thousands of Greek mercenaries were loyally serving the Persian kings.

The Greeks took their success badly. The following century was filled with wars between Greeks. This period was called the Peloponnesian War, and it weakened the major Greek cities (especially Sparta and Athens, the major contenders). Sparta emerged the winner, but by 371 B.C., other cities, led by Thebes, displaced Sparta. But the fighting continued, with Persia skillfully subsidizing the losing side so the wars would go on and Greece would get weaker.

Finally, in 355 B.C., Macedonia appeared on the scene in the form of Philip, the heir to the shaky throne of Macedonia. Philip was nearly as amazing as Alexander. While Philip was the heir to the throne, there were several other contenders, and Athens and Persia were backing the others. But Philip moved fast and skillfully and quickly consolidated his control. This impressed the Macedonians, Greeks, and Persians. But Philip was to do a lot more, much to the consternation of everyone.

Philip was an original thinker. He completely reorganized the Macedonian army, which had previously been little more than a feudal levy the king could call out to defend Macedonia, or hired as mercenaries to pursue the king's private purposes. One of Philip's first moves was to seize control of the most productive gold mine in Greece. This gave him an income of a thousand talents (about twenty-four million 1997 dollars) a year. With this he could afford to keep a professional force of soldiers on duty at all times. But around this core force of some ten thousand troops, he introduced new weapons, training, and tactics.

Philip had been exposed to extraordinary generalship while a teenage hostage (a common situation in those times) in Thebes. There he saw revolutionary tactics and military organization that led to the crushing of a Spartan army in battle. This defeat was a rare event for the well-trained and determined Spartans. Philip observed, learned, and carried his lessons back to Macedonia.

Philip proceeded to use his new army to smash the barbarian tribes surrounding, and usually threatening, Macedonia. His flair for diplomacy led him to turn many of these tribes and kingdoms into loyal allies. Philip then went to take on the Greeks. A series of campaigns and some adroit politics turned Philip into the leader of a Greek (save for Sparta) coalition, whose main purpose was the invasion of Persia and the permanent liberation of the Greek cities in Asia Minor. But just as this campaign was about to begin in 336 B.C., Philip was assassinated. Alexander became king, and his biggest problem was not military or political, but fiscal.

A major difference between today and Alexander's time was the primitive state of the money economy back then. There were no central banks, and anyone with precious metals, the proper artisans, and an attitude could mint his own currency. Many kings, cities, and major merchants did just that. Although the coinage came in many different flavors, there were two very common denominations.

The "talent" (mentioned in the Bible) was about sixty-five pounds of gold, silver, or whatever. It was the weight a human porter could comfortably carry over a distance. The talent was used as a means of settling major accounts between merchants and governments. Throughout this chapter we will refer to the Euboic silver talent, worth some $24,000 in 1997 money. This is a tricky valuation and to better understand it let us consider the money for day-to-day use, when the talent was turned into coins.

The most common coin was the drachma (further divided into six obols). A talent of silver would produce six to eight thousand drachmae, depending on who was doing the minting. For simplicity's sake, let us use a four-dollar (six thousand to a talent) drachma. A laborer working for cash wages would earn twenty to thirty drachmae a month, the same wage as an infantry soldier (who could also get a lot more in loot). A painter (who did pictures on walls) made about six times as much. A teacher of language, literature, and mathematics made about eight times as much and a teacher of rhetoric (which included formulating arguments and then delivering them effectively) got ten times as much as a laborer.

What could you buy with one drachma? One pint of good quality wine. Better-quality wine cost 50 percent more. For one drachma you could also buy half a pint of fresh olive oil, about nine ounces of pork, or some seven liters of wheat, millet, lentils, split peas, or dried beans. The above items, plus sundry veggies (even cheaper) comprised the bulk of the diet. One could eat well, by the standards of the time, for three obols a day. Lodgings cost a bit less. But most jobs came with meals, so you only had to spend your own money on wine and a place to sleep.

Clothing wasn't cheap. Work boots cost five drachmae a pair. The rest of one's clothing cost about the same. The economic situation in ancient times was not unlike what exists in Third World countries today. Your average ancient Greek could not buy a portable radio or any other gadget, but there were luxuries one could indulge in, such as musical instruments and jewelry. And there was always a lot of wine, and sweets made with honey. Prostitution flourished, as did gambling and betting on athletic contests.

A talent could also buy the services of ten to twenty mercenary soldiers for a year.

THE CHALLENGE

The principal problems Alexander faced were economic. Alexander had a magnificent standing army, one of his father's major achievements. The army had grown in the years before Philip died, from ten thousand to over thirty thousand. The army's cost now exceeded Philip's income. He had been making up the difference with plunder and extortion during his wars with the Greeks. But now those wars were over, and the troops still expected to be paid regularly. Alexander noted how the funds could be obtained by invading Persia. He was in a situation similar to Saddam Hussein's in 1990; Iraq had a large army, couldn't afford it, and next door was wealthy Kuwait.

Alexander was no Saddam Hussein, however. Alexander won most of his battles and was a much more beneficent ruler. Alexander inherited a debt of nearly thirteen hundred talents and a monthly payroll of three hundred talents. His monthly income was less than two hundred talents. He had to go forward with the Persian invasion or lose his troops. Without his army, he could lose his head, as the Greek cities might decide to settle the "Macedonian Threat" once and for all. He knew the Persians had thousands of talents that could be seized by a successful conqueror. True, no one had done it before, which seemed to make it more of a sporting proposition for Alexander.

Alexander's Greek coalition, most of the Greek colonies and Macedonia, had a total population of some four million people. The Persian Empire had twenty million. The annual cash income of the Persian king was over ten times what the Macedonian king received. Worse yet, the Greek world knew what Persia was all about, and all agreed it would not be a pushover.

THE SOLUTION

Alexander was aware that his father had produced an army that performed with deadly efficiency. Alexander had a decisive advantage with such an army. And he knew the Persians were unaware of exactly what they were up against. Alexander was also taking advantage of a new Persian king who had just come on the throne. The civil war accompanying the arrival of the new king had weakened Persia. Moreover, Greeks in Persia had been reporting that the normally efficient Persian civil service had, over the last few generations, gotten a bit stodgy. Persia was not all it appeared to be. A young vigorous king, backed by a formidable army, could march in and take it all. Alexander sold his vision to the rest of Greece, just as his father had done (just before he was assassinated), and, in 334 B.C. marched off to Persia with thirty-five thousand troops. He left ten thousand behind to keep an eye on Sparta and any other Greek cities that might develop their own vision. Alexander had a payroll to meet.

During his campaigns against Persia, Alexander's solutions to his financial problems showcased a wide array of talents.

★ Strategic vision. While Philip's planned invasion of Persia was actually quite modest (simply liberating the Greek colonies and taking some interior lands), Alexander upped the ante. He wanted it all. Alexander knew that simply tearing off a chunk of the empire would simply make the Persians mad and eager for revenge. But if the entire empire were conquered and Hellenized (infused with Greek culture), Greeks would be immeasurably stronger, and their principal enemy would be gone for good. Alexander thought big, logically, and followed up on his visions. One can see the same thing happening when a smaller company eventually absorbs its larger competitor. More commonly, the smaller company takes its larger rival's customers. It can be done, Alexander was doing it twenty-four hundred years ago.

★ Systematic solutions to problems. Like his father, Alexander systematically attacked tricky military and political situations and in the process fashioned well-thought-out, and often seemingly counterintuitive, solutions. A perfect example of this was the manner in which Alexander conducted his invasion of Persia. The Greeks came by land, ferrying troops across the Turkish straits (by Byzantium, now Istanbul.) As he expected, his first opposition was from the local satrap (Persian governor). Alexander easily won this battle (at Granicus), even though half the Persian troops were formidable Greek mercenaries. Alexander knew it would be a while, nearly a year, before the Persian king off to the east could assemble a larger army and come after him. So in the meantime, Alexander attended to another problem. The Persian fleet in the area was more powerful than anything the Greeks could assemble. Decades of Greek fighting Greek had allowed the Persians to gain this naval supremacy. So Alexander had to defeat the Persian navy using only his army. The solution, to Alexander, was obvious—conquer all the ports along the eastern Mediterranean that the Persian ships depended upon for supplies. Sailors had to drink and eat, and the quantities of food they needed could only be obtained from the large port cities. Most of the Greek ones were already on Alexander's side. The hostile towns would have to be taken. And so, for the next year, Alexander captured one port city after another. Many cities simply surrendered, and so did the Persian fleet when they saw what was happening. Alexander then began going after the interior towns. He promised lower taxes and more lenient rule. The people of Asia Minor were tired of the Persians and either warmly accepted the Greeks or simply renounced their Persian overlords and submitted to the Greeks. When the Persian king Darius showed up in 333 B.C., Alexander won another victory at Issus (Alexandretta, in Turkey). Alexander knew the next Persian army would wear itself out marching all the way from Iran to the Mediterranean coast, so he let the Persians come to him. Thus, rather than pursuing the Persians back to their bases in modern-day Iraq and Iran after the battle, Alexander continued to take possession of other Persian lands in the Middle East. He went to Egypt, took over, and founded the city of Alexandria. While he was doing this, the Persians had spent a large amount of money to bribe several Greek cities (including Sparta, which needed little encouragement) to rebel against Macedonia. Alexander had anticipated this, and had left one of his fathers best generals, Antipater, behind with ten thousand well-trained troops. Antipater made short work of the rebellion, then sent nearly half his force to Alexander in Egypt, knowing his king would need all the troops he could get for his final battle with the Persian king. In 331 B.C., Alexander moved toward Babylon (Iraq) to fight the final battle for control of the Persian Empire. Darius had already offered Alexander everything west of Babylon if he would make peace. No deal. Alexander wanted it all, and he was willing to gamble all to get it. In 331 B.C., Alexander met and defeated a Persian army four times larger than his own. The Persian king escaped once more, only to be murdered by some of his demoralized followers. The empire was now Alexander's. It took four years of heavy campaigning and systematic application of solutions to problems no one had ever solved before.

★ Thorough preparation. Alexander's father was a fussy fellow who demanded thorough preparation and surrounded himself with like-minded people. Alexander embraced this approach, and nowhere does it show up more strikingly than in the way he managed logistics. Keeping an ancient army fed and supplied was no easy task. Then, as now, logistics was the key to successful military operations. Each soldier needed two or three pounds of food a day, otherwise they got cranky or too weak to fight. Unless you had a very disciplined army, each soldier would have one or more camp followers (servants, girlfriends, etc.) who also had to be fed. It was common for there to be ten times as many camp followers as troops. While horses and oxen could eat grass, they preferred to do so in daytime, and it took many hours of grazing to get their day's nutrition. Thus you had to move very slowly to allow the animals time to graze, or else feed the horses grain, which could be eaten in less than an hour. But you needed ten to twenty pounds of grain per animal per day, which had to be carried or obtained locally. Such was logistics in prerailroad times. You actually couldn't carry much food with you, because the animals carrying it would have to eat a portion of it each day to keep going at a reasonable pace. Allowing the animals to graze slowed you down. Speed was an advantage in a campaign, and speed required a lot of food. A pack animal, in effect, can carry a ten-day supply of food for itself. Same thing for humans, although if you eliminate weapons and other equipment, a twenty-day supply can be carried. Put simply, an ancient army could only carry a few days' worth of food with it. For the most part it was dependent on locally obtained food supplies. Alexander got the best of the situation in two ways, both demonstrating his ability to prepare thoroughly for a situation. First, he sharply limited the number of camp followers traveling (and eating) with the army, just as his father had done. He was able to do this, allowing only one or two camp followers per soldier, because his troops were highly trained and well-disciplined professionals. This had taken him and his father years to accomplish. But it paid off when the army was in the field, where it could move faster and consume less in food supplies than any Persian army. Secondly, Alexander established an intelligence and diplomatic service to scout the route the army would take and arrange to purchase food from the locals. These advance men had earlier determined which routes would yield adequate food supplies. Alexander's logistics experts could also arrange for ships to bring food to the army at prearranged points on seacoasts or along rivers. Alexander's supply arrangements are still studied by military historians as an example of what ancient armies were capable of in this area. Thorough preparation was a habit with Alexander, and he applied it to everything he did.

★ Hire the best. A commander is only as capable as his subordinates, and Alexander took full advantage of the talent pool ancient Greece provided. While most of his key military commanders were Macedonians, schooled in the meticulous techniques his father Philip had pioneered, highly educated Greeks were taken on for technical and diplomatic chores. Alexander even organized teams of scientific researchers to study what Persia had to offer and quickly adapt it for the army's use. To make all this work, Alexander had to recognize talent and be able to reward those who succeeded and dismiss those who failed. This Alexander did throughout his career. When Alexander died, his empire broke up. But able men, Alexander's men, were able to keep several successor kingdoms going for several centuries. The Greek influence in the former Persian Empire lasted longer, and some of it remains to this day.

★ Communications. Even before modern mass media arrived in the nineteenth century, Great Captains realized the value of getting their message out and letting word of mouth do its work. Alexander saw to the public-relations angle, writing his own press releases, as it were, in his official letters to the folks back in Greece as well as carefully crafted directives for his new Persian subjects. In his own lifetime, Alexander was much admired and well thought of. This was largely due to these primitive, but effective, public-relations efforts. Alexander also took a team of historians with him on his campaigns, which is the main reason we know so much about what he did and how he did it.

★ The common touch. Macedonian aristocrats were noted for their common touch. They mixed easily with their subordinates and looked down on foreign nobles who dressed lavishly and set themselves apart from their people. These Macedonian customs allowed Alexander to obtain enormous loyalty from his troops. Even the Greeks, who expected their leaders to puff themselves up a bit more, tended to warm to Alexander once they had worked with him. Alexander aided this process by adapting his leadership style to something the Greeks were more comfortable with. What helped him most with the Greeks was the democracy practiced in most Greek cities. Alexander went after Greek voters like a seasoned politician. You cannot take power for granted. You are not given authority—at best you get an opportunity to exercise it for a while.

★ Physical and psychological courage. For a warrior, courage was not just an asset, it was a necessity. Alexander inherited his father's mental courage, but outdid his sire in physical courage. Alexander thought it normal to place himself at the head of key attacks. Although wounded many times, he survived all these fights by carefully selecting, training, and inspiring several hundred men who comprised his personal bodyguard and elite strike force. When Alexander flung himself into the thick of battle, he was not making a reckless decision. He knew such moves would inspire his entire army, and he was confident his companion cavalry (bodyguards) would fight, to the death, by his side. Alexander was brave, but he survived this habit by not being stupid about it.

★ Cultural awareness. Alexander's vision was one of cultural, not just military and political conquest. Although a Macedonian, Alexander had fully embraced Greek culture. He felt it was not enough to just conquer the Persian Empire; he had to infuse it with Greek thought (Hellenize it) and thereby turn the many cultures of the Persian realm into long-term allies. To do this he had to be aware of how these other cultures worked and thereby develop measures to make Greek culture acceptable. As a keen student, Alexander absorbed details of the peoples he conquered and was quick to promote able foreigners to positions of authority. He encouraged Greeks in his army to take foreign wives and founded over fifty cities and peopled them with Greek settlers and locals. In addition to providing loyal colonies in foreign lands, Alexander knew these new settlements would be an ideal means to spread Greek culture and thought. Most of these new cities survived and many still exist. Alexander's conquests lasted so long because he planned it that way and systematically did all he could to realize his long-term plan. Modern managers encounter the same problems during mergers or acquisitions. The firm being "conquered" usually has its own culture and become rather unstable if a new culture is imposed. Alexander, a twenty-four-hundred-year-old executive wearing armor and wielding a sword has a lot to teach his pin-striped counterparts of the twentieth century.

★ Situational awareness. Perhaps the greatest of Alexander's skills was his ability quickly to size up a situation and promptly take the most effective action. This skill has been called many things over the centuries, but the contemporary expression is situational awareness. That term came from research into what made a few pilots aces (shooting down five or more aircraft), while most were either victims (getting shot down) or survivors (avoiding getting shot down, but not doing much damage to enemy aircraft). It was discovered how aces shared an ability to sort out quickly a rapidly changing situation (as in air combat) and just as quickly make the right moves. Further work showed it was possible to develop what little situational awareness skills most of us have. Alexander had the situational awareness talent, and he managed to surround himself with many others who shared that trait. High performers in many fields still do this, whether they be currency traders or basketball players.

Alexander, with all his natural talent and acquired skills, was obviously a remarkable leader and manager. Examining his many skills in detail provides useful lessons for the modern manager. Alexander took a promising situation and leveraged it into a spectacular success. Alexander was not perfect, of course. He was a king and often acted like one. He could be sneaky and rather brutal at the ancient version of office politics. But, then, whether a trait is a vice or a virtue depends on where one stands and what century one comes from. Alexander learned, from an early age, how necessary it is to hustle and struggle to accomplish anything. When still a youngster, he noted that his father had sons by other women, and wondered aloud to his father if he, the firstborn, was sure to have the throne. His father gave him some unsettling, but very useful, advice:

"Well then, if you have any competitors for the kingdom, prove yourself honorable and good, so that you may obtain the kingdom not because of me, but because of yourself."

Although Alexander died of a fever, probably malaria, in 323 B.C., many of his accomplishments lived on for centuries. Within two hundred years of his death, Rome conquered Greece, Macedonia, and many territories to the east. But within six hundred years, all that remained of the Roman Empire was the eastern, Greek-speaking part. Many isolated tribes in the back country of Afghanistan still speak admiringly of the foreign conqueror Alexander, who came by long ago and did what no one has done before, or since, defeated the Afghans.

CHAPTER 3

★ JULIUS CAESAR ★

THE GREATEST COMMUNICATOR

WHILE CAESAR IS thought of as a successful general and ambitious politician, his greatest asset was communication. Both in writing and in person, as an orator or debater, Caesar deliberately molded public opinion and motivated his armies in a way not seen again for nearly two thousand years. How Caesar did it will sound familiar to inhabitants of our media-intense age, and Caesar's techniques are still valid.

Julius Caesar is perhaps one of the most unsympathetic characters of our study. This was a man who lusted after raw power and would do almost anything to obtain it. After studying Caesar's life one can only conclude that Machiavelli used Caesar as his role model for *The Prince*. Unlike Alexander and the other generals in the book, Caesar was not raised as a warrior. He took to the battlefield out of necessity and late in life to gain the political power he desired.

THE WORLD OF CAESAR (100–44 B.C.)

The Hellenistic world Alexander created would thrive for a century and a half until conquered itself. Its eventual downfall would not come from the east, where Alexander had directed all his efforts, but from a bunch of upstart farmers to the west. Rome, a small city surrounded by numerous farms, had slowly grown in strength for three and a half centuries since its founding in 753 B.C., and then began conquering its neighbors. The Romans had first been a kingdom, but had discarded the monarchy in 509 B.C. They then developed a republic based on examples of city democracy they had seen in the Greek colonies of southern Italy. Their republic was an ongoing process over the centuries, and it got more complex as time went on. The Romans developed a series of assemblies for electing citizens to different city offices. Power in Rome was, unlike the custom elsewhere, distributed among several notable citizens and not controlled by a single king. Somehow they were able to make it work, even though there was a constant power struggle between the wealthy families (who tended to get elected to most of the offices) and the mass of the population (who provided most of the voters, and the troops for the army). Put simply, voting power was based on wealth, and there were regular censuses to determine who was worth what. The wealthy few could not just vote themselves into power continually, but needed a portion of the votes from the rest of the population. Thus the elections for the various city offices were hotly contested as different factions from the wealthy families sought the votes of the people. Once a Roman held one of these offices, he was entitled to join the Roman senate for life. As complex as the Roman system was, it was amazingly responsive and enduring. After the republic disappeared in the late first century B.C., there was not another democracy like it for over a thousand years.

The Romans were not only democratic, they were very aggressive. They defeated and absorbed their Italian neighbors one by one. By the 200s B.C. they were in contact with the mighty Carthaginians of North Africa and the warlike tribes of mineral-rich Spain. After a century of fighting, they conquered both of these areas and were ready to turn their efforts east.

In the mid second century B.C. the Hellenistic world was not the power it had been under Alexander and his successors. Macedonia was no longer the glue holding the Greek states together. Rome became involved with the Greek states first by helping them defeat Macedonia and then slowly bringing all the other Greek states under Roman rule. By 148 B.C. the Romans were the Microsoft of the Mediterranean. However, this laid the groundwork for the downfall of the Roman Republic.

By 133 B.C. the seeds of the Republic's destruction had begun to take root. The army of the Republic had always been made up of citizens of Rome who owned property and could afford to equip themselves as infantry soldiers. But while the Republic increased its reach across the Mediterranean, the wars the citizen-soldiers fought in were farther away and lasted longer. In the early Republic, a legionnaire would be called up to fight his neighboring Italians for a month or so and then return to his farm. Now with the fighting taking place in far-flung places like Greece, Spain, and the Middle East, the common soldier might not return for years.

When the veteran did return he often found his land had been bought cheaply by one of his richer neighbors. The wife or elderly parents of a soldier would borrow money from a wealthy landowner to tide them over a bad harvest, an avoidable disaster had the military-age men been around. Even if his land or a portion of it was still intact, the soldier-farmer's life was not as appealing as before. So the poverty-stricken legionnaire would move into the city. As a result, his descendants were no longer landholders and not eligible for the army, although they could serve as rowers in the navy.

Another effect of the wars was the increased use of slaves by the Romans. The many successful wars yielded soldiers and civilian captives who were auctioned off to the rich. In previous times, wealthy Romans could only cultivate as much property as they, their families, and those few Romans they could afford to hire, could work. With the abundance of cheap slave labor, the rich could now farm ever-greater tracts of land. The rich began to push the smaller farmer off his holdings. More people flowed into the cities, causing the number of landless citizens to grow at an alarming rate.

Between 133 and 121 B.C., Rome went through a period of unrest where two different noble factions formed and struggled for power; the *populares* (those for the people and reform) and the *optimates* (those for the elites and the status quo). These two factions continued to struggle with each other for the next several decades. But while the Roman elites were busy squabbling, things were not going well in the provinces. In 113 B.C. two Germanic tribes rolled across southern Gaul, destroying several Roman armies before halting on the northern border of Italy. Numidia (Berber tribes in North Africa) also became a problem. The Numidian conflict allowed a young and successful general by the name of Marius (156–86 B.C.) to make a reputation for himself.

Marius reformed the Roman army and, in doing that, made possible Caesar's rise to power. First, Marius did away with the property requirement to serve in the army. Second, he offered higher pay and promised land grants to the soldiers after successful campaigns. The result was an army composed of men with a more mercenary and less public-spirited attitude toward military service. But the soldiers were still Roman citizens, and the incentive system Marius established was also directed at getting soldiers out of the army and onto their own farmland. This was generally considered a good thing.

Because of these reforms, and Marius's leadership, the Republic was saved from external threats. But he also brought the Republic closer to extinction, for soldiers increasingly owed their allegiance to the generals recruiting and paying them, not Rome.

Marius's rise to power as consul did stop, temporarily, the civil unrest in Rome. He was even forced to put down a revolt started by former *populares* supporters of his. Marius retired from public life in 100 B.C. Ten years later he was called out of retirement when all of Italy broke into war over the issue of non-Roman Italians becoming Roman citizens. He and another general, Sulla (138–78 B.C.), were able to settle the affair, defeating the other Italians militarily, but granting them Roman citizenship to avoid future conflicts. Soon after the "Social Wars" were over, the two war heroes came into conflict. Sulla was an *optimate* and Marius was a great favorite of the *populares*. A dispute over who should command an army arose. Sulla won, and Marius fled into exile. Sulla tried to bring things under control using great violence, killing or sending into exile any who opposed him. Problems in Greece and Asia Minor then arose, forcing Sulla to leave Rome to deal with them. As soon as he left, the *optimates* and *populares* were at each other's throats again, literally. Almost ten thousand men died in the fighting. The rioting in Rome encouraged Marius to return and regain his lost power. Marius raised an army to accompany him back to Rome. Inspired by Sulla's violent solutions to these political problems, Marius took bloody revenge. Soon most of Sulla's friends were dead or had fled. Sulla, meanwhile, had his hands full in the east and could not rush back to Rome when he heard about Marius's return. Sulla did eventually return to Rome with his army. The revenge of the *optimates* began as Sulla marched his troops into Rome. When it was all over, anyone posing a threat to Sulla was dead or in exile. For the next few years Sulla ruled with an iron fist as dictator (the official kind, recognized by Roman law). Sulla promoted many lower-ranking Romans, and even some foreigners, into the Roman ruling class, so great were the losses among upper-class Romans. As a practical matter, the Republic was, if not dead, certainly not anything like what it used to be. Because of the Social Wars, most Roman citizens now lived outside Rome. The rules for allowing these new citizens to participate in the governing of Rome were unclear, and many of the traditional leading families of Rome were decimated by the recent civil wars. A vacuum was created with Sulla's retirement from the dictatorship. It was a vacuum looking for ambitious new leaders to fill.

THE CHALLENGE

Caesar was born into turbulent times, with the whole Roman system undergoing a revolution. Young Caesar's biggest challenge was to survive the changes. The "downsizing and layoffs" of this period did not mean you merely lost your job; it could mean you lost your citizenship and would be exiled to a lonely rock in the Mediterranean, or your life could be forfeit.

Caesar's ambition knew no bounds. This was not unusual among wealthy Romans, but Caesar was exceptionally ambitious as well as remarkably talented. The challenge for him was that raw ambition could lead to an early death if he was not careful. He had to pick and choose his political battles carefully. His rise to power had to be carefully plotted. One misstep could result in his exile or execution. But he could not appear as a weakling. The Romans had no stomach for the weak. He had to appear strong, but at the right times and for the right reasons.

Another challenge for Caesar was his family's background. He had been born into a noble family with an illustrious genealogy. But they did not have the one thing Caesar needed most, money. The Romans still had a class system recognizing some families as members of the ancient aristocracy. But the class given most recognition was made up of those families that had produced rich and politically successful men. His full name, Caius Julius Caesar, said it all. Caius was his given name. Julius was the name of his clan (an illustrious one) and Caesar was his particular family (producer of many prominent Romans) within the clan. Caesar had the bloodline; all he needed was a credit line.

The ability to flourish in the political environment of Rome required huge sums of money. Entertaining was a big part of climbing the power ladder. Entertaining in these times did not mean inviting a few business associates out to dinner. The public demanded large celebrations to be held in Rome. You entertained as many of the four hundred thousand Roman voters as you could. The aristocracy demanded that elaborate feasts be held constantly for themselves, while the common folk wanted chariot races and gladiatorial contests. Caesar's family did not have money to fund these types of events. It would be necessary for him to find ways to entertain the voters.

Another challenge Caesar faced was enlisting the help of those around him. Because of the complex nature of the Roman political system, no goal could be achieved by one man. Caesar had to rise to the top with the help of many allies, mentors, and followers.

Born in 100 B.C., Caesar spent his early years doing what most ambitious upper-class Romans did. He served with the army, on diplomatic service, and received the Roman equivalent of a college education (majoring in logic and rhetoric). He belonged to the *populares* faction and was related to Marius. His first public service was at age sixteen, when he entered the priesthood of Jupiter. In Rome, there were many priestly orders, but they were as much political as religious positions. Sort of like being a Mason in later centuries. In 81 B.C. he was sent on a diplomatic mission to Asia Minor (Anatolia.) Then he had to deal with the dictator Sulla. But he managed to escape the wrath of Sulla, mainly by leaving Rome for an extended period. In 75–73 B.C. he distinguished himself in military campaigns against Mediterranean pirates and other enemies of Rome in the east. Thereafter, he began to run for public office. By 69 B.C. he had entered the Senate. Through the 60s B.C. he pursued further public offices and distinguished himself as a military commander in Spain. He became consul in 59 B.C. He also forged an anti-*optimates* triumvirate with Crassus and Pompey, and together they controlled the government. This led, as a reward, to his five-year proconsulship in Gaul.

This was to be Caesar's opportunity to get rich, and he did so with gusto. Caesar brought all of Gaul under Roman rule in a series of brilliant campaigns. He spent most of the 50s B.C. in Gaul, getting richer and building his army of loyal veterans. Caesar's army made his political enemies back in Rome nervous. So in 49 B.C., the Senate ordered Caesar to disband his army and come home, alone. Caesar refused and marched his legions toward Rome. Thus began a civil war lasting four years, although Caesar seized control of Italy within the first year and ruled Rome by himself until his assassination in 44 B.C.

Caesar always reached for the top position in Rome. He developed an impressive bag of tricks to help get him where he wanted to go.

THE SOLUTION

Caesar managed to scramble to the very pinnacle of Roman society using a brilliant assortment of techniques, all of which are still applicable today.

★ Networking. Caesar's method of networking is not one recommended for today, but the theory holds. The implementation just needs to be different. According to contemporary sources, Caesar was quite attractive to women, the John Kennedy of his time, so to speak. He used his looks to seduce the wives of many of his enemies and, also, those of some friends. Caesar was also suspected of using sex any way he could to further his career. All his life, Caesar denied he had a homosexual affair with an eastern king while on a diplomatic mission as a young man. This led to the saying that Caesar was, "the husband of every woman and the wife of every man." Hmmm, maybe not all that different from the politicians of today. The unique thing about Caesar's relationships was how the women seemed to remain loyal to him even after he lost interest in them and moved on to the next domestic conquest. The result of these liaisons, beyond the obvious hedonistic ones, was that Caius Julius had influence in almost every quarter of his political world. It also allowed him to gain knowledge obtainable no other way.

★ Mentoring. Caesar, being from a relatively poor family, needed money to advance his career, and he largely solved this problem early on by becoming the protégé of Crassus (115–53 B.C.), then the wealthiest man in Rome. Crassus was a good businessman, but less skilled as a politician. So it was not difficult for Caesar to arrange to further the political goals of Crassus in return for financial backing. Caesar, in turn, mentored many other younger Romans, some of whom turned up to assassinate him in 44 B.C.

★ *Carpe Diem* (Latin for "seize the day"). Caesar was an accomplished opportunist. He never failed to take advantage of apparently opportune situations, and even some inopportune ones. An example of Caesar's opportunism was his being elected to the office of *pontefex maximus*, a religious office, in 63 B.C. It brought stature and connections beneficial to Caesar in his political career. It also brought with it a large house in a better part of town, thus Caesar could entertain the elite who would bring him power. Caesar jumped at the chance to gain the office even though it meant, if he lost, possibly getting run out of the city by those who opposed him. Caesar had no deep religious feelings himself, and he was criticized for his energetic election campaign for this religious position. But the highest religious office in Rome was merely one step along the way to his ultimate goal.

Another event illustrating Caesar's opportunism was how he divorced his wife, Pompeia. A few years before Caesar started his political career, he had married Pompeia, a granddaughter of Sulla. This was a marriage of pure convenience. First, it gave him a favorable standing with the *optimates*, Sulla being the favorite son of the *optimates*. Caesar needed to be seen as friendly to the *optimates*, as all his family ties were with the *populares*. Secondly, it gave him money which at the time he needed badly. The marriage, over the years, had grown inconvenient as Caesar strengthened his affiliations with the *populares*. In 62 B.C. Caesar was elected praetor. A responsibility of this office was to hold a yearly religious celebration in his house. The celebration was conducted by the Vestal Virgins, and all men were banned from it. This time the celebration did not go as planned. A prominent Roman by the name of Clodius disguised himself as a woman and entered the house. He was discovered, and a scandal resulted. Romans took sacrilege seriously. Moreover, there was a rumor that Clodius had invaded the party to make love to Caesar's wife, Pompeia.

Caesar had to step very carefully here. Crassus, the current political power and Caesar's benefactor, admired the daring of Clodius and bribed the jury to get him acquitted of sacrilege. But based on the rumor of Clodius's designs on his wife, Caesar divorced Pompeia, thus getting rid of his inconvenient wife. The problem now was, because of Crassus's admiration of Clodius, he could not say outright that Clodius had been at the party to seduce his wife. So, seizing one opportunity had given him a new problem. When asked why he had divorced Pompeia he replied, "Caesar's wife must be above suspicion." With these clever words he did not offend Crassus, yet did not deny Clodius was at the party to seduce his wife.

★ Communication. The Pompeia affair says much about Caesar. It demonstrates how he was a master communicator. With one sentence he simultaneously showed support for his current leader and still disparaged the man who offended him. This is but one example of Caesar's ability to communicate. Caesar lived in a time in which skillfully wielded words were often mightier than brute force. This operated on several different levels. For example, one way a young man climbed the political ladder was to prosecute other aristocrats in court. To the Romans this was a game. It was not really important what the charges were, or even whether one was successful in one's prosecution or defense, as it was common for rich defendants to win their cases by bribing the juries. The point was how one could turn a Latin phrase. The more persuasive an orator, the more respect one gained from one's peers and the faster one's career went. From the very beginning of his career, Caesar excelled at oratory and rhetoric. He always had the talent, and when things got hot in Rome for him during his early political life, he left to go study rhetoric at Rhodes (a noted center for this).

Cicero considered Caesar one of the finest orators of his time. One of the secrets of Caesar's oratory was, he kept it simple. If he felt a word would not be understood, he did not use it. Cicero praised him for his precise use of Latin. Moreover, Caesar managed this even though he had a high-pitched voice. Even the Romans preferred a good bass or baritone for public speaking, but Caesar overcame this.

Not only was Caesar a spellbinding orator; he was also a skilled writer. Instead of letting a historian, or someone else, tell the story of his campaigns and victories, he told the story himself from his perspective, using his interpretation of the facts. Although his books are not the best-written books on war (they were deliberately written for a mass audience), they are above average and let him get his message out to the people the way he wanted it to. Caesar understood that if he did not tell his own story, someone else would tell it for him. He wrote his history of the Gallic Wars as they were going on and sent the manuscripts back to Rome to be copied and distributed. In Roman times, letter writing was considered an art on the same level with writing books today. Letters were shared, then saved and reread. There was no printing, and the "books" produced were handwritten and then copied by professional scribes (often slaves, but expensive slaves). Most Roman citizens were literate. If someone wrote a compelling book or public letter (posted in public places), it would be widely read and hand copied. Caesar realized the impact of literacy on Romans and, more than any other Roman, took full advantage of it. Between his speeches, public-relations stunts (he put on great games), and writing, Caesar was the first user of multimedia campaigns to sway public opinion.

★ Alliances. Without proper alliances Caesar would have not gotten far in his political career. Caesar made, and unmade, numerous alliances during his career. One, however, was more important than the others. Around 70 B.C., an ally of Sulla—Crassus—came to power. Crassus lacked leadership skills but he had something no amount of leadership could make up for in Rome, money. Lots of money. Crassus was an able businessman and the richest man in Rome. Crassus was able to accomplish his goals by working through others with better political skills. Caesar was the opposite of Crassus, having an abundance of leadership skills but lacking wealth. Therefore, Caesar saw an opportunity to form a convenient alliance. Over the years Caesar served Crassus well and was able to strengthen Crassus's power base. Crassus rewarded Caesar by allowing him free rein with Crassus's money and supporting Caesar's election for various offices. At the same time Crassus was gaining power, another Roman, Pompey (106–48 B.C.), was also climbing the political ladder. Pompey had led several successful military campaigns, made a lot of money for himself and Rome in the process, and helped Crassus defeat the revolt led by the gladiator Spartacus. For this he was held in high esteem by the Rome oligarchy. There was one little problem—Crassus and Pompey did not get along. Caesar could not afford to ignore Pompey, who was after all basically a competitor. Whenever possible, Caesar supported Pompey's initiatives without stepping on Crassus's toes. Ultimately, Caesar cemented his alliance with Pompey by arranging the marriage of his daughter to Pompey. Soon Crassus put his doubts about Pompey behind him and the three were able, in effect, to rule Rome as a triumvirate for a while. It was amazing how Caesar was able to bring the three of them together. But this one action made it possible for Caesar to take over Rome himself. Eventually Caesar outmaneuvered Pompey, militarily and politically. And Crassus had the good sense to die at the right time, thus avoiding a falling-out with Caesar over who would be first in Rome.

★ Motivation. In order for Caesar to lead the armies for his Gallic campaigns and then the Civil War, he had to motivate the troops to follow him. Caesar seemed to know instinctively what motivated men, and he used this ability to good effect. As Caesar stood poised to lead his men into Italy and on to Rome at the beginning of the civil war, he had to motivate his men to follow him. He could have spoken of the need to defend Roman justice, he could have talked of the plunder they would receive if he took power. But he knew this would not motivate the men of Rome. Instead he talked to them of honor. He spoke of how the Senate had dishonored their general by attempting to remove him from command. Caesar understood that the legions would feel his dishonor meant their dishonor, too. If he was out of power, their promised postarmy rewards would not follow. He did not have to mention this to them. He appeared to appeal to their higher nature, while at the same time motivating them with more down-to-earth matters. His legions followed him to Rome, fought to defeat Pompey, and enabled Caesar to become dictator.

★ Follow the money. Caesar died the richest man in Rome, worth eight hundred million sesterces (nearly a billion dollars in today's money.) Caesar was only wealthy at the end of his career. Before, he was always scrambling for funding. Growing up in the Roman form of genteel poverty, he always had to depend on others for financing. He made it a point to let people think he was rich, and then hustle every sesterce (about a dollar in today's money) he could to keep ahead of his debts. It was the financial backing of Crassus that got Caesar through his early political career and financed the four election victories leading to his year as consul. When Caesar got his proconsular appointment to run the Gallic provinces, he really didn't need Crassus anymore. Caesar picked up (and quickly spent) several hundred million sesterces during his nine years (58–50 B.C.) in Gaul. Meanwhile, Crassus went off to Iraq to fight the Parthians (Iranians) and died there in 53 B.C. This was fortunate for Caesar, as he owed Crassus big time for all those loans and "gifts." Moreover, he owed Crassus favors as well as cash, and Crassus was the one person to whom Caesar was most indebted. The untimely death of Crassus at the hands of the Parthians was one of those fortunate events people like Caesar come upon more frequently then the rest of us. When Crassus died, he was the richest man in Rome and worth 170 million sesterces. Caesar needed more money than that to keep up his military government in Gaul. In 51 B.C. he had eleven legions, all of them raised and paid for out of his own pocket. Rome expected the provinces to pay for the Roman legions protecting them, and kept them in line.

A freshly raised legion had about six thousand troops. It cost five to ten million sesterces to get a legion started (weapons, equipment, uniforms, etc.). It then cost another ten million sesterces a year to keep the legion going. Caesar's army was costing him over a hundred million sesterces a year, thus he was always short of money. One reason Caesar refused the Senate's order to return to Rome alone, and lose his control over Gaul, was because he was, as always, in debt. But in Rome there were hundreds of millions of sesterces he could use if he controlled the city. So Caesar crossed the Rubicon River and entered Italy an outlaw. But in short order, he was the law. His first move was to loot the three temples in Rome holding cash reserves for emergencies, grabbing about a hundred million sesterces. He grabbed cash anywhere he found it during the next four years to finance his side in the Civil War. Thus, when he was assassinated, Caesar was finally a rich man. Dead, but very rich—the richest man in Rome and the first Roman billionaire.

In the end Caesar was not able to escape his time. No matter how opportunistic he was, no matter how many alliances he created, the oligarchy was always there. The oligarchy had always been frightened by anyone who said he was for the people but was actually intent on wielding power alone. So even those who said they were *populares* in the end were *optimates*. With Caesar, Rome passed from five hundred years of democracy, however limited it was by twentieth-century standards, to five hundred years of one-man rule, and gradual ruin. Rome had grown great when the Republic flourished. The golden rule of this period was, as the Romans put it, "what affects all, must be decided by all." Caesar was not the only cause for the Republic's destruction, but he was the principal one. It was a case of magnificent talents applied to disastrous ends.

CHAPTER 4

★ CHARLEMAGNE ★
THE GREAT ADAPTER

CHARLEMAGNE WAS AN eighth-century autocrat who was not reluctant to make deals rather than just have his own way. This was what made him great and what created a political unity in Europe not seen since. Although known largely as a tireless warrior, which he was, he spent more time mending fences and building bridges than he did breaking heads. Looking formidable and acting conciliatory was a style Charlemagne created and from which modern managers can profit.

Over six feet tall and in robust health, Charlemagne looked like a king. This was a period when such appearances were even more important than they are today. Self-confident, energetic, and inventive, Charlemagne was one of those rare conquerors who died, in bed, as an old man. He was able to look back on a life of accomplishment, of victories gained more by ideas than force.

THE WORLD OF CHARLEMAGNE (A.D. 742–814)

This was the Dark Ages, the period in European history after the fall of Rome and before the Renaissance. It wasn't all that dark, as we shall see, but it was rather a low point in the history of European civilization. Economically, things weren't much different than they were in ancient Greece or Rome. Politically, well, there were no democracies. That would take several centuries to reappear. Indeed, there was less government in the Dark Ages than in the preceding centuries of Roman rule, which was one reason things were so, well, dark. Three centuries after the Roman Empire collapsed in the west, the Roman times were fondly remembered as the good old days.

Roman culture had not completely disappeared, but it had been greatly overlaid with the tribal cultures of the Germans, who had moved in and taken over the Roman territories. By Charlemagne's time, the Germans had been in charge for some four centuries. Charlemagne himself was king of the Franks, arguably the most successful of the German tribes.

The Franks started out, five hundred years before Charlemagne, as a confederation of tribes. Tired of being dumped on by other Germans and by the Romans, they came together in the third century A.D. and adopted the common name "Frank" (derived either from the word "free" or "spear"). The Franks managed to stay independent during the chaos leading to the fall of Rome, and even lent a hand at finally defeating the Huns at the Battle of Châlons (A.D. 451).

Living alongside the Romans in Gaul for several generations, the Franks absorbed the lessons of Roman civilization and developed their own organized kingdoms. In the fifth century, with Roman authority gone, many of these Frankish kingdoms were united under Merovich (reigned 448–458). His grandson, Clovis (reigned 481–511), tidied up the frontiers a bit and also converted to Christianity. Thus organized and united, the Franks systematically conquered southern France and large parts of Germany. So successful were the Franks in their nation building that all Germanic peoples became known to non-Europeans as "Franks," the Arab version being, for example, "Ferengi." One part of the Frank nation, France, carried the original name into current times.

The Franks were keen to use Christianity, an educated clergy, and Roman methods to run their kingdom. But at the very top, the manners were German. The key concept of feudalism, the surrender of personal freedom in return for protection and material well-being, was a combination of German and Roman practice, and was most developed and most widely practiced by the Franks. The Roman feudal practices were older and had grown up in the frontier areas where refugees fleeing into Roman territory had to surrender freedom for protection. The Germans, entering Roman areas now stripped of central government and the Roman army, found defenseless people willing to accept the same terms.

The Germans had long followed the practice of every able-bodied adult male being trained and employed as a warrior. This idea had long since died out in Roman areas, where even recruiting soldiers for the regular army had become increasingly difficult. The Germans were as wolves among sheep in these Roman lands. It was a large-scale protection racket, with the Germans, even after they blended into the population and lost their language and German customs, still forming the core of the feudal warrior class. This may explain why so many knights were blond and blue-eyed.

A key element of feudal life was known as the "Manor System." This was nothing less than a company town largely owned and completely controlled by the local noble. This fellow might be a knight or some higher-ranking aristocrat. The manor was an area over which the noble ruled and supplied such vital services as justice. Some areas still had the Germanic jury system, others simply had the local lord holding court and being judge, jury and prosecutor. The lord often owned, or controlled, key services like milling grain, ironworking, or even baking bread. If the lord didn't own these facilities, he charged a fee for their use. The Germans found that the Romans had thoughtfully set up manors for them, in the form of large, self-contained farming communities owned by wealthy Romans. This was an ancient Roman practice, as it was considered the most efficient way to invest one's wealth. The farms were worked by slaves or tenant farmers, and the Germans took them over, turning the workers into serfs. The Germans had nothing against slavery, it was just that they, like the Romans, found serfs (semifree slaves, in effect) more productive than slaves. The Franks, under a series of competent kings, turned the Roman estate practices into what became known as the Manor System. European slavery survived into the seventeenth century.

By the eighth century, the heavily armed, and increasingly armored, Frankish warrior on horseback had demonstrated his superiority over any infantry force in Europe. It is likely such cavalry forces would have fared poorly against Roman legions trained and disciplined in the classical manner. But the Romans had forgotten about training and lost their discipline before the Germans overran the empire. It would be another five centuries before an effective infantry army was again created (the English yeomen and the Swiss pikemen of the thirteenth century). Thus for five centuries, from the 700s to the 1200s, the man on horseback ruled the battlefield. But only if you had a lot of them.

These knights were expensive. The horse, arms and armor cost a minimum of twenty thousand 1997 dollars, and usually a lot more. Annual repair and replacement cost several thousand dollars. Even more expensive was the training, about ten years' worth, at some five thousand dollars a year. Then, for the ten to thirty years the knight was capable of fighting, supporting him would cost at least five to ten thousand dollars a year. But it got even more expensive when knights married and had a family to support as well.

The economic system had changed little since Alexander's time. The principal currency was still a small silver coin, in this case the denier. Worth about $1.50 in 1997 money, it was the same as the medieval English pence (240 equaled one pound sterling, a system surviving until 1970). Charlemagne's pound (of) sterling (silver) was called the livre. A major problem in this period was the multiplicity of people minting coins with the same name. The weight and value of the denier varied, with some worth a dollar (or a little less) and others close to two dollars. Just to complicate matters a bit more, the Germans preferred silver coinage, the Italians preferred gold.

But it all came together in the eighth century, as the kings, especially the Frankish kings, realized they could use the Manor System, now staffed with self-sufficient knights, to produce a system providing trained soldiers for the crown and also providing reliable men in local positions of authority throughout the kingdom. Some of the German nobles who adopted this system, especially the ones in former Roman lands, realized that it was basically an adaptation of the third-century Roman system of giving the large-estate owners government authority over their lands and people and the responsibility for raising troops.

Never forget that the Germans, until they settled down, were basically an army with families attached. War was the central element in their lives. They kept herds of animals, practiced primitive agriculture (which exhausted the soil and forced them to move) and hunted. But the favored form of economic activity was a successful war and the loot it would produce. Roman lands were always seen as rich, and when the Roman defenses declined, the Germans simply took advantage of an opportunity they had been waiting centuries for. Once they settled down on Roman land, these military fellowships became the basis for long-term political relationships.

The Frankish kingdom culminated in Charles the Great (or Charlemagne in French, or Karl der Grosse in German). Since 628, Charlemagne's ancestors had held the office of "Mayor of the Palace," a sort of Shogun to a series of increasingly feeble Merovingian kings, running the country in the name of the crown. Pepin the Short (reigned 751–768) ended the line of the inept Merovingians by sending the last one to live out his life in a monastery. Pepin made himself king of the Franks, and everyone agreed this was a swell idea. Pepin may have been short, but he was also very persuasive.

Given the usual customs of the time, Pepin practiced an exceedingly civilized way to change dynasties, sending the deposed king into exile rather than just killing him. Pepin's son was Charlemagne (reigned 768–814), an all-around competent fellow who made things happen. Charlemagne expanded and organized the kingdom. He spent most of his warm-weather time leading his armies. His winters were spent administering his realm and encouraging scholarship. As a reward for helping the pope out against some Lombard (a German tribe settled in Italy) enemies, in 800 Charlemagne was crowned Roman Emperor, initiating the so-called Holy Roman Empire. Charlemagne's kingdom, at its height in the early ninth century, encompassed all of France, Switzerland, Belgium, and Holland, as well as most of Germany and parts of Spain, Czechoslovakia, Austria, and Italy. But that empire didn't last, no matter how well it was run. The German practice was to divide the father's holdings among his sons, although it often happened that one of the brothers would, by negotiation or force, bring all the family holdings back together. This is how the Frankish kingdom survived intact until Charlemagne could have it all. But Charlemagne himself had the misfortune to have one surviving son who himself had four sons who were unable to keep the empire united. During the ninth and tenth centuries, Charlemagne's empire basically divided into two parts, German and French. The French half (most of present-day France) was quite Romanized, and most of the population spoke dialects of Latin. The German half spoke German, and still does. The 842 document making this division official, the Oath of Strasbourg, was written in German and French in recognition of this division.

THE CHALLENGE

When Charlemagne became king of the Franks in 768, his first challenge was his brother, Carolman, who shared the throne. It was an unfortunate Frankish custom giving all the king's sons a share in the empire. Each son either got his own kingdom, or had to share rule with another brother. It was several centuries before most European kingdoms adopted the custom of primogeniture (the eldest son got the crown all to himself). While the eldest son might well be a dolt, this at least eliminated the fragmentation of power and civil wars usually resulting when several sons survived a king. Fortunately, Charlemagne's brother died in 771, leaving one king of the Franks.

Charlemagne inherited an enormous realm, full of cultures with diverse languages, laws, and customs. In A.D. 800, Europe contained some twenty-nine million people and Charlemagne controlled nearly half of this population. But when Charlemagne started out in 768, he had only some six million subjects and many restive and powerful neighbors. Charlemagne had simultaneously to deal with the diverse subjects he already had, while coping with hostile Saxons, Bavarians, Moslems, Lombards, Avars, Byzantines, and Vikings (just to mention the major ones).

The Germans had proven themselves capable conquerors, but by A.D. 800 Charlemagne found himself with the largest German empire to date. But he had no proven and reliable techniques to keep it going. Something had to be done before the whole thing collapsed (a common occurrence with previous German conquests).

While all this was going on, the knowledge and technology of the Romans was receding farther into memory. This period was, with reason, called the Dark Ages. The rather more primitive culture of the Germans had destroyed Rome and was only slowly picking up, and recycling, the pieces. The Catholic Church was doing what it could to collect Roman documents and knowledge, but some major assistance was needed to recover the wisdom of the ancients before it disappeared for good.

THE SOLUTION

Charlemagne put together a collection of techniques unique for leaders of the Dark Ages. To someone from the twentieth century, Charlemagne's solutions seem contemporary. But in the ninth century, Charlemagne's techniques appeared extraordinary. Thus Charles became Charles the Great (or Charlemagne in French), one bright light in the otherwise dimly lit Dark Ages.

★ Military competence. Charlemagne was one of the more able military commanders to emerge from the wreckage of the Roman Empire. Charlemagne spent much of his reign at war, unifying the miscellaneous kingdoms and duchies of what are now France and Germany, capturing lands from the Slavs in the east, beating back the Muslims in Spain, and curbing the Lombards in Italy. These military obligations could not be ignored, for Charlemagne lived in a violent period. Many people saw war as glorious and necessary work. It was also more entertaining than slaving away on a farm, as most of the population did. There was no shortage of young lads willing to take their chances on the battlefield. But Charlemagne was not interested in hordes of ill-trained, poorly equipped, and difficult-to-discipline teenagers. Charlemagne relied primarily on professionals, namely his mounted warriors, who were beginning to look like the medieval knights that still capture modern imagination. Charlemagne's soldiers weren't quite knights yet. Their armor was more leather than metal, and they still preferred the sword to the lance. But Charlemagne had seen the Lombards use mounted lancers to good effect, and promptly adopted many Lombard techniques. Charlemagne's Franks and the Italian Lombards were both Germans, but the German tribes had been wandering all over Europe for half a thousand years by now and had picked up widely divergent social and military practices. Eventually, the Lombards in Italy and Franks in France were absorbed by the local populations. This made these German populations much less warlike. Only in

Germany did the Germans remain completely German in language and customs. But in this period, the Germans were all over the place and eager to try new things, especially if it involved organized violence. Charlemagne was a good example of this attitude.

To his opponents, Charlemagne's signal technique was speed. He moved his troops about with uncharacteristic alacrity. He often gained victories solely through these rapid maneuvers, avoiding battle while a perplexed enemy army fell apart trying to match Charlemagne's speedy marches. The purpose of all this activity was to threaten key cities and regions his foe depended on for support (food and fresh troops). Frankish warfare also relied on pillaging enemy territory and terrorizing the local population, an ancient custom and major factor in getting the troops to serve. Think of it as a primitive bonus system. Since most of Charlemagne's foes were tribal kingdoms, who drew their troops from the general population, this threat to family and home would demoralize poorly disciplined tribal levies.

In addition to speed, Charlemagne was a remarkable tactician, who always seemed to be able to make the right move on the battlefield. Charlemagne came from a long line of capable tacticians and he proceeded to develop his talent further through study and practice.

★ Logistics. Charlemagne was not only interested in fewer, more capable troops; he was also aware of the logistical aspects of warfare. Armies tended to live off the land, meaning they plundered the local population. This was fine if one was in enemy territory, but caused problems when one's troops stole food (and often much else) from the locals in nominally "friendly" territory. The friendlies could turn hostile real quick once they had been pillaged by a passing army. Charlemagne eliminated this problem by organizing supplies for his troops and punishing those of his lads who got out of hand. This was easier said than done, but Charlemagne had the knack for disciplining warriors without ticking them off permanently. Part of this was due to Charlemagne's track record, a long and successful one. Another persuasive argument was Charlemagne's physical stature. He was a big guy, built like a contemporary football running back. In a time when disputes were likely to be settled out back with fists or long swords, being able to stare the other guy down instead was a useful talent. Charlemagne had the talent. He was also king. So Charlemagne tended to get his way with a minimum of fuss or permanent bad will.

Like Alexander's and Roman logistics before them, Charlemagne's depended on planning. Charlemagne was always surrounded by clerks and sundry experts. Charlemagne had a love of knowledge and expertise. Charlemagne's staff calculated the supplies required for a campaign, then sent messengers armed with the king's authority, and cash, to buy the supplies needed and have them ready for the troops. Many of these skilled assistants were clergy. While it is true most of the educated people in this period were clergy, Charlemagne also knew men of the cloth were less apt to betray him or become distracted. Clergy were less likely to be molested while traveling, and most clergy spoke Latin, the universal Church language, enabling easy communication with foreign clergy.

Charlemagne's logistical problems were mitigated somewhat by the custom of letting the troops freely plunder once in enemy territory. This was considered an essential part of warfare and solved a lot of supply problems once you entered enemy lands. The pillaging made the troops happy, sort of like letting employees keep their frequent flyer miles, saved the expense of buying supplies, and encouraged the enemy to give up the fight.

★ Tolerance and flexibility. Charlemagne ruled over peoples speaking dozens of different languages with even more sets of laws and customs. An ancient error rulers made was to try and force all their subjects to use one body of laws and customs. Charlemagne did not do this. Rather, he respected local practices and went so far as to write them down as much as possible. Many of the tribes he ruled over were still largely illiterate and passed on their laws and customs orally. Charlemagne's efforts to get all these things written down impressed the locals with their king's interest in their welfare. Writing down all the local laws had enormous practical use when settling disputes between people of two different groups. He instructed his judges first to establish which set of laws the participants in a legal action should be tried under. This went a long way toward getting people to accept the king's justice. This was a major achievement for Charlemagne, as he knew that one reason the Romans had successfully ruled a hundred million people was the peace and justice they provided. Even today, those nations growing their economies most quickly do so because they have a workable and fair legal system. Charlemagne provided the peace with his armies, and the rule of law via his corps of judges schooled in dozens of different legal systems.

Charlemagne could also be brutal, a technique he used when he felt more tolerant methods had failed. Charlemagne tended to favor the carrot over the stick, despite his annual military campaigns. For this reason, when he died, his subjects remembered the tolerant Charlemagne more than they did Charlemagne the warrior.

★ Administration. Charlemagne created a flexible and responsive administration for his empire, creating duchies and counties, and appointing competent officials to run things. What made this feat all the more admirable was that it was done within a feudal society, with the mounted warriors Charlemagne was so dependent on maintained via grants of land (and the people on them). The warriors ran their little fiefs like a business, charging the farmers rents and levying as many taxes and fees as they could get away with. The profit from these activities provided the warrior with the means to arm himself and buy horses. When he answered the king's call to war, he went off with a few servants and lesser warriors, and horses for everyone. Charlemagne appointed the larger landowners to be rulers of provinces. For those areas adjacent to hostile tribes, he gave the local rulers additional powers and financial aid. Selection of provincial rulers was a critical task, and Charlemagne did it very well. Many of his contemporary kings were less capable in this department and ended up with poorly administered provinces and subordinates who tended to be disloyal and dangerous to the king.

Charlemagne also owned hundreds of estates (villages or towns and the surrounding farmland). He appointed teams of auditors, usually a clergyman and a learned layman, to travel about inspecting the royal properties and reporting back to the king. These *"missi dominici"* ("messengers of the lord") also checked in on the local officials running the province and the warriors living off their own estates. In this way, Charlemagne always had timely reports on how his own properties were doing, as well as conditions in the kingdom as a whole. Naturally, the mere presence of the *missi dominici* tended to keep everyone honest, or at least fearful of having their scams uncovered. The *missi dominici* system began as a rather modest effort to check on the king's property, but was expanded during Charlemagne's rule into a rather extensive system of auditors. This was not a new technique, but was used over a thousand years earlier by the Persians, and several other empires since.

★ Education. Charlemagne organized schools on a large scale, importing scholars from other regions with the promise of patronage. He eventually found time to learn to read as an adult. Illiteracy had not bothered Charlemagne much in his earlier years, but he led by example, and learning to read was his way of showing how important education was. Promoting education was an uphill fight, for many of Charlemagne's nobles were rough warriors of the old school, who looked down on anyone who could read. The king was thought eccentric, if not a little soft in the head, for surrounding himself with all those scribes and scholars. But Charlemagne knew knowledge had made Rome great, and he noted how the Christian Church grew ever more powerful because of its near monopoly on education and books. Church-controlled monasteries contained most of the libraries (a few hundred books was a big library) and the skilled scribes who could make handwritten copies of books. Charlemagne drew out the Church scholars and encouraged them to support his program of widespread education. Charlemagne wanted literate laymen and aristocrats. He got them.

★ Economic development. Charlemagne may not have been able to read as a young man, but he could count, and he saw the importance of commerce, industry, and trade to the health of his kingdom. The impact of his economic reforms was immense, as it created far more wealth and economic opportunity than the region

(Europe outside of Italy and Spain) had seen in several centuries. Charlemagne standardized the currency, as well as weights and measures. Well, he didn't standardize these things as we know the term today. But in an era where there were many different values for what a foot, bushel, gallon, or silver coin represented, standardization was a welcome change. When the Roman Empire fell in the fifth century, this standardization was one of the casualties. Charlemagne encouraged trade and new technologies. The Church was in the forefront of scientific experimentation, because it had access to most available knowledge, and Charlemagne saw to it that this knowledge was shared with the laypeople who could best use it.

After his death, Charlemagne became the center of a complex cycle of myths and legends rivaled only by the tales surrounding King Arthur. But Charlemagne was real, not a myth. His accomplishments were a monumental milestone in the history of managing large organizations. In an era lacking electronic communications and reliable transportation, Charlemagne made things work in a timely and reliable fashion. While Charlemagne had the advantage of a long tenure, his policies could have been pursued by a succession of leaders. Basically, Charlemagne demonstrated the value of consistently adapting to a wide variety of situations rather than trying to impose radical solutions quickly. Charlemagne took his time, moved deliberately, and got results.

There's a lesson in all of that.

CHAPTER 5

★ GENGHIS KHAN ★

THE MASTER OF SPEED IN ALL THINGS

THE MONGOLS, NOMADIC warriors of Central Asia, were united under Temujin (Genghis Khan) in the thirteenth century and proceeded to conquer most of Asia and parts of Europe and the Middle East. The Mongols' principal tool was speed, speed in all things, on and off the battlefield. The Mongols were also masters of organization, discipline, communication, and rapid decision making. That their system lasted several centuries tells you there was more to it than a temporary military advantage. The myths coming down to us portray the Mongols as a bunch of wild, undisciplined barbarians. This is utterly false, for the Mongols did what they did using world-class management techniques. There are lessons to be learned here.

THE WORLD OF GENGHIS KHAN (1162–1227)

Temujin ("blacksmith") was the given name of the man who was eventually proclaimed "Great King" (or "Genghis Khan" in Mongolian.) Temujin was born into a culture that had lived in the saddle for thousands of years. The Mongols were the eastern group of pastoral tribes occupying central Asia from Manchuria to southern Russia. Always have, and still do. A warlike and rugged bunch, the tribes constantly raided and fought with each other. But their favorite prey were the more settled, and less violent, peoples to the south. The only good news in all this was the smaller, much smaller, number of central Asian nomads compared to their more civilized southern neighbors. When

Temujin was born in 1162, the population of modern-day Mongolia (and the area to the north containing Lake Baikal) was only some eight hundred thousand people. These were the Mongol tribes, intermixed with some Turks. To the west were the larger number of Turkish tribes, containing some three million people. Centuries earlier, the Turks and Mongols were the same people. But they had been evolving since in different linguistic and cultural directions. From the ninth century, the Turks had been moving west, and by the twelfth century were in control of much of the Middle East. Both Turk and Mongol still shared many customs and cultural traits, thus many of Temujin's "Mongol" warriors were actually Turks. A few generations after Temujin's death, most of the "Mongols" were literally Turks, although some of these Turks had adopted Mongolian language and customs.

The nomadic tribes of Central Asia had long threatened their more numerous and settled neighbors. In the fourth century B.C., the Huns (Mongols/Turks before the split) had invaded China. Eventually repulsed (in part by the newly built Great Wall), they turned west and in the fourth century A.D. showed up in Europe, hastening the fall of Rome. Other Central Asian tribes moved west, including the Magyars, who left their language (and genes) to present-day Hungary. A related tribe settled Finland, also leaving their language behind. Many other tribes came and went.

The Central Asian nomads lived off their herds and were fiercely independent. Government was via clan and tribal leaders. The Turkish tribes established larger-scale governments once they moved into areas more suitable for farming and city living. This is what always happened when the nomads successfully moved off the plains. But no one had ever organized all of the nomadic tribes from the great plains of Central Asia. No one had ever been able to master the entire military might of the Central Asian tribes. No one until Temujin.

THE CHALLENGE

Although born into a family of the Mongol "nobility" (families recognized as "blessed" by the gods to produce tribal leaders), his father was killed by a hostile tribe while Temujin was still a child. He and his family thereafter lived on the run and out of luck until Temujin came of age. When Temujin did grow up, he had several items on his agenda. The first one was regaining his family's place in Mongol society. His second item was of larger, much larger, import. Temujin wanted to be the one to realize the yearning of all Mongols for as long as anyone could remember. He wanted to conquer the world.

For centuries, the Central Asian tribes had dreamed of conquering the settled lands beyond the plains of Central Asia. The nomads' life was hard, and it was known that beyond the plains, especially to the south, in China, there was more wealth and an easier life. All this could be had, if only the tribes had a leader strong enough to hold them together and lead their massed might to wealth and glory. Temujin had what it took and quickly began demonstrating his wide range of skills.

First he gained control over his own tribe. Starting with a few thousand followers, faced with competition from over half a million hostile fellow Mongols, Temujin applied a ruthlessness his fellow Mongols could understand and appreciate. While Temujin's initial goal was control over potential Mongol rivals, his main objective was to take the tribes farther than they had ever gone before and make his followers rich. Yes, the Mongols were motivated mainly by wealth and glory. What had held them back so far was their inability to stop fighting each other and the lack of a leader who could get all the Mongols to march to the same music. This was akin to herding cats. Possible in theory, but heretofore impossible in practice.

Those peoples who bordered the Central Asian plains always expected more raids. When a new leader came to power, it wasn't unusual for an occasional large army to erupt from among the nomad tribes. But no one expected what Temujin was about to unleash. Not even his fellow Mongols.

THE SOLUTION

Temujin knew what he wanted. He wanted it all, and he moved fast to get it. By 1185 he became khan (king) of his immediate tribe. He suffered one of his few losses in battle two years later and spent the next seven years as an exile, mainly in China. The Chinese had long welcomed, and supported, such exiles and used them to keep the

Mongols fighting each other rather than invading China. Temujin used the Chinese more than the other way around. Over the next ten years he systematically defeated, and absorbed into his army, the Mongolian tribes. In 1206, the Mongols proclaimed him Genghis Khan; the supreme king of the Mongols and, as the Mongols understood it, everything they could conquer. Temujin then began working on the Turkish tribes. By 1210, with many of the Turks under control, the Chinese realized they had contributed to the creation of a force they could not control. The heretofore cordial relations between Mongols and Chinese soured. The following year, Temujin advanced into northern China. No Central Asian tribe had ever conquered China before. Temujin had a few million people under his control, and he was going after the three large kingdoms comprising China. More to the point, Temujin was attacking over a hundred million Chinese. It would not be done in a year, or a few years, but over two generations. Temujin laid down the foundation for a system that was able to keep his conquests going for another two centuries of conquest.

What set Temujin apart from earlier tribal conquerors was a collection of skills and techniques which are worth studying.

★ Incentives. Temujin realized that for all their talk of glory and adventure, what could really motivate the Mongol (and any other) warrior was loot. There wasn't a whole lot to steal on the Central Asian plains, except for livestock, horses, and women protected by equally nasty nomads. These the tribesmen stole from each other constantly. Temujin offered the prospect of immense quantities of goodies from beyond the thinly populated plains. By organizing exceptionally large Mongol armies (up to a hundred thousand warriors), he was able to battle his way into the thickly populated lands to the south and provide his troops with riches undreamed of. Temujin kept an eye on the newly acquired wealth and who got what. He knew the booty could cause squabbling among his troops and was careful to make sure he grabbed enough for himself to provide a financial reserve for times when the soldiers were in a bad mood and he needed to be generous. The discipline of his troops ensured that the looting was done in a systematic manner, at least by contemporary standards. While loot kept the troops going, he used another currency to bargain with enemies and potential allies—life itself. The Mongols were famous, or infamous, for giving opponents an offer they found hard to refuse. When Temujin came upon a new tribe or city, the standard offer was—complete and instant surrender, or total obliteration. Entire cities and tribes were killed when they resisted. When word of this technique got around, many otherwise stout opponents thought it over and submitted promptly. This particular incentive also did much to ensure continued loyalty, for those who later crossed Temujin were soon visited by a Mongol army with orders to loot and kill. No further negotiation was allowed. One crossed Temujin once, and one was dead.

★ Loyalty. This was a traditional principle, followed only selectively by the central Asian tribes. One was expected to be fiercely loyal to members of one's family, and to a lesser extent to one's clan and tribe. But beyond that, anything was possible, and the usual result was treachery and an endless number of bloody feuds and animosities. Temujin overcame this problem by establishing a new form of loyalty extending beyond clan and tribe. By establishing himself as the Great Khan, Temujin was able to create a loyalty to himself and his officers that went beyond tribe. He further weakened tribal loyalties by mixing warriors from several different tribes in his military units. While some units were from the same tribe, these were usually tribes that had signed on to follow Temujin at an early date. As more non-Mongol tribes joined Temujin's army, the individual warriors, or small groups of them, were put into units of known loyalty or under the leadership of Mongol officers. Temujin still had to contend with family loyalties, but he used these family ties to his advantage. He would keep an eye on, and cultivate the personal loyalty of, key family members. Once he had those individuals securely in his debt, he could depend on the entire family to stay in line. If a loyal follower later betrayed this trust, he could expect only death for himself and, quite often, his entire family. The concept of forming new systems of loyalties is something useful to the modern managers operating in new forms of organizations. Multinational organizations and the increased use of electronic communication make it possible to form new loyalties and thus change the traditional system of loyalties.

★ Discipline. Mongol combat methods were adapted from techniques used in hunting. Mongols depended on hunting for much of their food, and hunting was considered a serious business. Strict discipline was taken for granted, and the leader of the hunt could enforce obedience with harsh punishments. This was carried over to Mongol warfare. Temujin institutionalized this traditional Mongol discipline throughout his entire army, adapting it to local customs as needed. Even though his troops were increasingly non-Mongol, the leaders of units tended to remain Mongols who knew how the discipline worked and how to enforce it. Executing a few errant troopers on the spot usually inspired the others, whether they were Turks, Chinese, Iranians, or Europeans. Few other armies at the time had soldiers as disciplined, and this gave Temujin's warriors a considerable advantage. Multinational managers would do well to copy this method of developing discipline. Not the executions, but the adapting of a proven system of discipline to local customs.

★ Political cunning. Temujin was, above all, an astute politician. Although his methods were basically those of a traditional Mongol chieftain, he was quick to size up the nuances of non-Mongol politics and take advantage of whatever political opportunities presented themselves. Temujin uncovered internal disagreements among his enemies and would deal with the contending parties to weaken his opponents before gaining their allegiance or destroying them. He made this work with Central Asian tribes and the more civilized kingdoms to the south. Knowing the potential foes were aware of the Mongol "surrender or die" policy, Temujin could deal with foreigners from a position of strength even when he didn't have a Mongol army in their neighborhood. As with most of his resources, Temujin made the most of what he had. This paid off particularly well in his political dealings with allies and enemies.

★ Speed. The most remarkable asset Temujin possessed was his use of speed in all things. The Mongols were known for their swiftness on the battlefield. But Temujin applied alacrity to everything he did. He did not waste time. Part of this was the impatience of a conqueror who wanted to subdue everyone in sight before old age caught up with him. But there was also the recognition that one could gain a tremendous advantage by moving faster than an enemy could, or expected you to. Although Temujin's earliest armies were all cavalry, he later used a lot of infantry. Still, he was able to move faster than his foes. This speed was the result of more than just the fighting style of the Mongol generals. There was also the discipline of the troops, their organization, and the planning capabilities of Temujin's officers. But speed had always been a key aspect of no-mad life. When hunting, and Mongols spent a lot of time hunting, speed was life. For the hungry hunter, inability to run down swift prey meant starvation. The Central Asian tribes also lived off their herds, and when the weather changed these herds had to be swiftly moved to better grazing areas before starvation or adverse weather began to kill them. Temujin adopted these ancient practices to his style of warfare. Speed, for the Mongols, was the difference be-tween success and failure on the battlefield. Modern managers would do well to pay attention to speed in all things. For this approach is one of the more successful of the twentieth century.

★ Organization. The Mongols had traditionally organized their ar-mies on a rational basis (as were many ancient armies). There were units of ten, a hundred, a thousand, and ten thousand, each with a leader and, in the larger units, a small staff. Temujin tinkered with this organization and made sure it was made a standard in all Mon-gol armies. This made it much easier to train officers and troops. The standardized organization meant a promising new commander could be sent to another unit and there would be no need first to learn how that outfit was organized. The standard organization also meant the same tactics worked the same way no matter which Mongol unit a commander was with.

★ Intelligence and communications. Collecting information (intelli-gence) and then getting information to the commanders needing it as quickly as possible. Temujin's intelligence system included spies and far-ranging scouts. This was not unusual for commanders of the time. What made the Mongol system especially effective was the communications setup, which was outstanding for its time. The nineteenth-century American Pony Express was similar. The Mongols established remount stations at twenty-five-to-fifty-mile intervals. Travelers possessing a "tablet of authority" (a handheld, inscribed, wooden panel serving as an official pass) could get fresh horses and supplies at these stations. This was most important for the individual riders carrying letters. When they tooted a horn before they reached the next station, a fresh horse and saddle would be waiting. Such a rider could cover over two hundred miles a day. Using fresh riders (a few were on call at each station) really important letters could cover over four hundred miles a day. This system allowed Temujin and his generals to control troops over an enormous area. Such a system also allowed Temujin to organize quickly a campaign using widely separate forces. At the time, most rulers depended on their spies or travelers from neighboring areas to give them warning of an enemy gathering forces for an attack. This ancient dependence on spies and interrogating traveling merchants no longer worked against the Mongols. Temujin could organize a major campaign long before the intended victim could get wind of it. Unleashing his armies on an unprepared enemy was yet another Mongol advantage. Normally, it took a local ruler weeks to assemble all of his troops from their farms and towns. When the Mongols hit without warning, the defending troops assembled piecemeal and were chopped to bits before they could put together a full-strength army. Thus Mongol speed multiplied the effect of Mongol armies.

★ Shrewd management of conquered territories. Temujin employed superior organization in his conquered territories. Think of it as exceptional management of divisions within a conglomerate. Using a small number of Mongol or Central Asian (Turks and others) administrators to keep an eye on things, he typically allowed local officials to run conquered areas. A Mongol garrison was stationed in key cities, and local troops were offered work with the Mongol field armies. Here, these non-Mongol troops could be on the winning side and share in the loot to be had when serving with a victorious army. The non-Mongol troops were usually infantry or siege forces. The Mongol cavalry would do all the running around and fancy footwork required to force an enemy into his walled cities. Then the non-Mongol soldiers would trudge in and take over the siege work. A siege could take months and involved a lot of digging and construction work. This was not the sort of chore mounted warriors enjoyed, so it was another example of Temujin's thoughtful organization of his forces. Even when fighting was not going on, Temujin used his rapid communications, extensive network of spies, and highly trained staff quickly to size up political situations and issue new orders more rapidly than most of his foes could respond. Speed was the key to Mongol success in all things, even management of conquered territories.

★ The right tools for the job. The Mongols were, from childhood, trained to be warriors. For most of them, their principal weapon was the compound bow. This weapon, in the same class with the longbow, was shorter and thus usable from horseback. And, like the longbow, it required over a hundred pounds of pull and a bowman trained to use it from childhood. While most adult males of the nomadic Mongol and Turkish tribes were competent bowmen, Temujin realized an army of nothing but archers would not suffice to win every battle against every possible opponent. Thus he expanded the traditional Mongol force to include more heavy cavalry (better-armored troopers using lance and sword to finish off enemy infantry.) As he moved into areas containing more cities and broken terrain unsuited for horsemen, he added non-Mongol infantry, engineers (for sieges), and sailors (for amphibious operations.) The earliest versions of gunpowder were used for cannon and rockets. Before the Mongols slaughtered all the inhabitants of a hostile city, they first sought out technicians and artisans (and exceptionally good-looking women) and spared them. The Mongols in general, and Temujin in particular, were always on the lookout for new technology and methods. This made it difficult for any of their foes to gain a technical advantage over the already very capable Mongol armies. Thus even in the allegedly backward medieval period, there was much technology to be had, and, in one of those historical ironies, it was the savage, "uncivilized" Mongols who took most advantage of it, making the Mongols the masters of adopting "best practices."

★ People skills. In common with all great leaders, Temujin knew how to deal with people. He was able to choose his friends, and enemies, carefully and accurately. Temujin was aware from childhood that errors in this area could be fatal. His own father was poisoned by "friends" in another tribe (the Tatars, which Temujin later exterminated, although their name lived on). It was relatively easy to deal with Mongols and Turks. Temujin know how these tribesmen lived and thought. But his real skill was in dealing with "civilized" people. Many of the cities and regions to the south quickly surrendered to the Mongol armies, and Temujin had to decide whom he could trust and whom he should execute or just keep a sharp eye on. It was essential to select effective and reliable administrators from conquered peoples, for there was no other way for the Mongols to keep on conquering and not run out of troops because of the need to leave garrisons behind. Although the Mongols used many non-Mongol troops, these could not be trusted to serve as garrisons and look after Mongol interests. Small Mongol garrisons were left behind, which served more as trip wires than anything else. If these garrisons were attacked by the locals, the small number of Mongol troops were usually wiped out. This made it clear to Temujin that he had to return and exterminate the local population. But Temujin preferred to keep the locals under control, and supplying money and supplies for his armies. So Temujin used his people skills to pick out those local notables who could run the place for the Mongols and do it efficiently and reliably. Temujin used the same skills to hire non-Mongol military leaders, diplomats, and key personnel of all kinds. Without this skill at dealing with people, the Mongol armies would not have gotten nearly as far as they did.

★ Ruthlessness. One must recognize that Temujin owed a lot of his success to his policy of mass murder and genocide. In this respect, the Mongols were even more bloody-minded than the twentieth-century Nazis and Communists. These latter two groups were responsible for killing over a hundred million people early in this century. That's quite a lot, and out of an average world population of 2.5 billion, it comes to some 4 percent. But the Mongols managed to kill nearly fifty million people when the planetary population was only 360 million. That's some 12 percent. The Mongols were three times as murderous as our twentieth-century butchers and that is the main reason the Mongols are still remembered as a rather ferocious bunch. Mass murder was another unfortunate fact of Central Asian life. Blood feuds were common. If one killed someone from another clan, that clan would want to return the favor to someone in one's own clan. So the only way to avoid an endless blood feud was to try and wipe out the other clan. Sometimes this took the form of killing all the adult males and taking the women and children into one's own families. But often enough, wiping out another clan meant killing everyone—man, woman, and child. Temujin used this ancient practice freely as he unified the Central Asian tribes under his banner. This ensured there was no one back home nursing an old grudge against him as Temujin went off to conquer the rest of the world. Then Temujin made wide use of this traditional Mongolian ruthlessness in dealing with those he wished to conquer. Those who submitted after a demand from Temujin were allowed to live. Those who resisted were wiped out. Anyone who gave him a really hard time, like a city stoutly resisting a siege, received the ultimate Mongol indignity. The city not only had its entire population massacred, but all animals were killed, the place was burned to the ground, and the Mongol troops were not allowed to loot. Everything was destroyed. Temujin rarely got that angry, and, indeed, he could not afford to as the troops saw the loot from a conquered city as their reward for the hardships of a siege. The Mongols quickly realized their ruthlessness gave them a great psychological advantage on the battlefield and at the negotiation table. Thus the Mongols never had any incentive to forsake their ferocious ways, and they never did.

★ ★ ★

★ Adaptability. A crucial aspect of Temujin's personality was his ability to adapt. Although Mongols, like all nomads, were quite adaptable, they did cling to certain ideas which, if not modified, prevented them from conquering anything but other nomads. For example, Mongols considered farmers to be, well, agricultural pests who ruined otherwise excellent pasture with their crops. Often the Mongols would slaughter these farmers simply to clear land so their herds could graze. At one point, the Mongols considered destroying all the farmers in northern China so the land could support more Mongol horses and herds. Temujin and his successors ultimately overcame their nomadic preferences and learned how to adapt to the ways of these more numerous farmers and city people. Temujin adapted constantly throughout his career. First he adapted to non-Mongol nomads (mainly Turks), then to Mongol and Turk peoples who had settled on farms and in cities. These he felt capable of trusting with key administrative positions, and he was largely correct. Temujin's children and grandchildren did the ultimate adaptation when they adapted well enough to rule the Chinese, Iranians, and many peoples in between.

Temujin died in 1227, just as he was preparing for another campaign to conquer all of China. His sons and grandsons completed the task for him. The military and political innovations of Temujin lasted for some two centuries. While some of his sons and grandsons were talented, not all were. What kept the Mongols going after Temujin's death was the system Temujin had left behind. It didn't take a genius to use many of Temujin's techniques. Ruthlessness came easy to the warriors of the Central Asian plains. The troops still had their speed, discipline, weapons, and other traditional accoutrements of nomadic life.

What eventually did the Mongols in was success. Although they had a fetish for "maintaining the old ways," no matter where they were, this became more difficult the longer Mongols lived outside of Mongolia. Life was easier in the south, whether it be in Iran or China. After a few generations of marrying local women and living the good life, the expatriate Mongols were no longer Mongols. Even those Mongols who went back to Mongolia were affected. These returning warriors often brought non-Mongol women with them, and the resulting children didn't act like Mongols (lacking a Mongol mother), and didn't look like Mongols either.

Moreover, the constant exodus of Mongol warriors from Mongolia actually caused the Mongolian population to decline. Temujin's victories were not bloodless. Most Mongol males from their late teens to at least their thirties would turn out for a campaign several times in their lives. Their biggest danger wasn't the enemy, but accidents and disease. The latter could be devastating. When the Mongols campaigned in southeast Asia, they would regularly lose half or more of their army to disease. Even under optimal conditions, 10–20 percent of the troops would be killed or maimed in the course of a successful campaign. There were only eight hundred thousand Mongols to begin with, and no more than a hundred thousand troops could be raised for a campaign. Many more non-Mongol troops were used, but the Mongols themselves also continued to suffer combat losses as well. As the wars of conquest went on year after year, more and more of the Mongol troops died, settled in conquered territory, or became invalids. It was another case of success spoiling the successful. The Mongols were unable to impress their lifestyle onto any other nations. The Mongol culture was unique to the Central Asian plains. Anywhere else the Mongols tried to establish their culture, they were eventually swallowed up by the more numerous local population. This happened where the Mongols set up shop in Iran, China, and elsewhere. Only in the vast plains of south Russia did the Mongols survive until the twentieth century. Here, the "Golden Horde" found an area remarkably similar to Mongolia itself and thrived, although they were eventually subjugated by the more numerous native Russians.

The Mongols saw nothing wrong with all this death and destruction. Their goals were conquest and loot. That they stayed to rule their conquered kingdoms was simply the Mongol way of keeping the loot coming. The Mongols were a very practical people, and Temujin knew how best to exploit that practicality. The Mongols were a prime example of how being good at something does not always result in doing much good for all concerned.

CHAPTER 6

★ EDWARD III OF ENGLAND ★
THE LBO KING

EDWARD'S ANCESTOR, WILLIAM of Normandy, had taken over England in 1066 by using, in effect, a leveraged buyout (LBO). This technique, issuing portions of the new territory to the warriors rather than dealing with bankers and brokers, was used by the descendants of William, down to the ninth generation, and Edward III, the monarch who was a political giant for most of the fourteenth century. Edward was a master of finance, politics, and war. He wove these activities together using techniques still useful today.

THE WORLD OF EDWARD III (1312–1377)

Edward III was born in 1312 and died in 1377. His mother and grandmother were daughters of French kings. This gave Edward reasonably firm grounds for claiming the French throne nine years after the male line of French kings died out in 1328. In 1327, at age fifteen, Edward was proclaimed King of England. Edward was not just mature for his age, he also had a very nasty family situation. Shortly before Edward became king, his mother and her lover had murdered his father, Edward II. This arose from a variety of reasons. Edward II was homosexual and a generally lackluster king. This was particularly noticeable in comparison to the previous king, Edward I (Longshanks). Edward II had the bad grace to appoint his untalented boyfriends to government jobs and generally carry on in a politically inept fashion. Edward II's principal failure was getting beaten by the Scots in battle. He was executed by having a hot poker shoved up his anus. This was not done in reaction to Edward II's homosexual proclivities, but because it was important that the deposed king appear to have died from natural causes (no visible signs of violence.) Edward III's subsequent coup in 1330 was a reaction by English nobles who saw yet another inept government. Edward III's mother was seen as a "French queen," giving out government jobs and patronage to her French friends and chums of her English lover. The English clergy, and many of the common people, were also appalled at the scandal of a wife overthrowing her husband the king, having him murdered, and doing all this in league with her lover. As bad as Edward II was as a king, the immoral ways of his French wife were seen as equally bad. Edward III sided with the English nobles and was mature enough to go along with the coup and then assumed the crown. He promptly executed his mother's lover and many supporters in interesting ways. His mother was not interfered with at all, but she was completely excluded from government, sent into exile in a remote castle, and died a happy, unrepentant woman.

Thus at an early age it was obvious Edward III possessed considerable political, diplomatic, government, and conspiratorial skills. He was also a remarkable warrior, being hailed as one of the premier knights of the age, as were his sons. There is a legend of a jousting tournament where several knights wearing nondescript surcoats entered the lists. They carried all before them, against some of the finest chivalry in England, and when the laurels were being handed out, they revealed themselves to be Edward and a couple of his sons.

Edward III was a large, good-looking man, as were all the Edwards. They looked like kings, which counted for a lot in those days. Being about six feet tall, he was considerably taller (by several inches) than the average noble of the period (and commoners were shorter still because of poor diet). Reportedly he had blond hair, but, if he followed the pattern of Edward I, this probably turned dark ("black" in some accounts) in his maturity and white in old age.

One of England's social problems in the early fourteenth century was that it was a German (Anglo-Saxon) and Celtic population ruled by French-speaking nobles. When Duke William of Normandy conquered England in 1066, he became king. But he was still a French noble and the duke of Normandy, (and a subject of the French king). Duke William also replaced nearly all the Anglo-Saxon aristocracy with French nobles. During the next two centuries, the French-speaking English kings acquired (mainly through marriage) even more property in France. Aside from marrying into each other's families, the French-speaking English nobility actively sought wives on the Continent. Finally, in the thirteenth century, a particularly able French king (Philip the Strong) took most of these French lands away from the English king. Thus by the early fourteenth century, only two French provinces, Gascony and Guyenne, were still ruled by the English king, and in 1337 the French king Philip VI demanded these provinces be returned to French control. The English king, Edward III, could ill afford to lose these provinces, as they were the source of most of his personal income. So Edward III challenged Philip VI's claim to the French throne, asserting that Edward III's claim (which did in fact exist) was superior. Thus began over a century of war, with Philip VI claiming the right to appoint French nobles as rulers of Gascony and Guyenne, and Edward III claiming he was the rightful king of France and England.

There were other issues involved. England had major financial interests in Flanders (the wool trade). To make matters more complicated, France supported the Scots in their wars against England.

While France had over three times the population of England, Edward had better troops, a more efficient government, and thousands of English soldiers who were more than willing to campaign in France and get rich in the process. Edward's biggest asset was the manner in which England had been administered by its Norman conquerors. William the Conqueror took control of England in 1066 and promptly calculated what he could afford to hand over to his "investors" (the warriors accompanying him on his conquest of England). Technically, William owned all he conquered. But, as with any leveraged buyout, the investors had to be compensated. In medieval terms, this was done according to the rules of the feudal system. Feudalism recognized the king as the owner of everything, but his "vassals" were given large territories to administer as if they owned them. The only "rent" they paid their king was military service. The degree of military service was worked out in detail via a written or oral contract. These "tenants in chief" of large landholdings in turn had their own tenants, who held smaller territories and owed military service to their overlord. These feudal lords also provided the legal and administrative services for their lands. The king served as the ultimate judge in the legal system and had the power to exact whatever taxes he could get away with. What made this system tricky was that the king really had no army of his own. He depended on the obedience of his vassals in delivering troops when called. If the king offended too many of his vassals, they could conspire against him and stage a coup. This would have happened more frequently than it did had it not been for the religious aspect of medieval life. The king was declared, by the Church and all practicing Christians, to be the anointed of God. So lesser mortals undertook attacks on the king with great reluctance.

THE CHALLENGE

Edward had two major problems. One was political. He had to rule a nation full of increasingly powerful nobles and a parliament constantly demanding power at the king's expense. This led to his second problem, which was financial. As king, he had to run the country pretty much out of his own pocket. He had the power to levy some taxes, but this wasn't enough. His only other source of income was "grants" from the parliament. The members of parliament tended to demand new rights in return for money. The parliament itself was a thirteenth-century innovation, created by the English monarchy to avoid a civil war and even further erosion of the king's power. The parliament was not a democratic one, but composed of the most powerful feudal lords of the kingdom. The major nobles (the "magnates"), senior clerics and representatives of the major towns, plus representatives from the shires (provinces) met and increasingly enforced the ancient Roman tradition that "what effects all must be decided by all."

But the king's major problem was always money. Money was the ultimate power, and the king never had enough of it. At the time of the Hundred Years' War, Edward required some $18–21 million (in 1997 dollars, with the medieval English pound sterling equal to $600) a year to run his kingdom. In wartime, the annual expenses rose to $30–48 million a year. In peacetime, Edward got some $5–10 million a year from taxes on the usually exempt Church properties. These required the pope's approval. As the popes were French during most of the Hundred Years' War, no more church taxation was allowed for the duration. Loans were used early in the war and varied each year from $7.2–12 million. Unable to pay back any of this debt, Edward defaulted on his loans in the 1340s, owing some $410 million. Without access to credit, Edward had to balance his budget by plundering French lands or imposing taxes on England. Rarely was he able to get more than $10 million a year in personal taxes out of England. So the English armies were forced to live off the (French) land, and this was a major factor in the war lasting for generations. The French lands were rich, and the English soldiers were good at pillage.

The GDP of England at the time was some $4–5 billion a year, so the tax burden of the central government was trifling by modern standards. But there were practical reasons for this. For one thing, there was less disposable income to tax in the first place. Tax too much, as some medieval rulers did, and your population shrinks from starvation, if they don't rise up in desperate rebellion first. But a more important reason for the low national tax was that government was largely local way back then. Centralized government requires more technology and technique than was available until quite recently. In the fourteenth century, the local lord, the original "landlord," was government for most people.

By Edward's time, the great nobles had developed a system called Livery and Maintenance, in which they hired hundreds, and sometimes thousands, of troops on a permanent basis. The "livery" referred to the uniforms they issued these troops, a custom that became quite popular with all aristocrats in the late-medieval period. The "maintenance" was the salary, or often just food and lodging, provided to these troops. Edward knew he was in for trouble when he saw some of these aristocrats showing up for parliament with hundreds, or thousands, of these uniformed retainers in tow. Edward needed a way to keep these magnates busy and out of his way, and the Hundred Years' War proved to be a useful distraction for several generations.

The Hundred Years' War not only kept the English nobility busy overseas, but also enabled a new wave of aristocrats to rise up. For the English, the war was all about money. Medieval poverty was deep and pervasive. Most of the population were farmers and got along on $1,000 a year (for the poorest) and about $3,000 (for the yeomen "middle class"). About 2 percent of the population did much better. These fortunate few ranged from the knights and esquires (fighting men or large landowners not knighted) who had incomes of $5,000 a year and up (as high as $100,000 or so) to the junior grade nobles, who took in $100,000 a year (but rarely more than a million). Most of these fellows were on the make; otherwise, they would not be doing as well as they were.

While the king enjoyed an annual income over $20 million, a few of the major magnates brought in as much as $7 million a year. The average magnate had only $1 or $2 million annual income to play with, but this was enough to maintain a substantial military force. Maintaining troops for a year under livery and maintenance rules would cost about $4,000 for each man. Hiring mercenaries for a campaign was much more expensive, mainly because these lads knew they were immediately being put in harm's way and demanded, and got, much higher wages than the livery and maintenance trooper. A mercenary force like this would cost from $2 million (a thousand men, plus camp followers) to $10 million (five thousand troops) for the three-month campaigning season and also included specialists for siege work, plus clerks and priests.

Armies tended to be small, not just because of the expense, but because it was difficult to feed a large force in a time when the roads were poor and transportation difficult. When there was a large army, it tended to be a feudal host, called up to perform feudal military obligation. These armies had a lot of poorly trained and equipped troops in them and were usually poorly led. Such armies were often defeated by smaller and more professional forces. Many of the battles of the Hundred Years' War were of this type, with the French feudal hosts being taken apart by the smaller but more capable English armies.

The situation faced by Edward III was the same one faced by all the kings of Europe (and elsewhere). As economies grew stronger and local nobles had more money to play with, these aristocrats increasingly used their military power to defy the central government and the king. This was an epic struggle of the medieval period, played out in all parts of the world. Those nations in which the central government prevailed grew strong and rich. In areas where the nobles maintained their independence (Germany and Italy, for example), unification didn't arrive until much later. For Germany and Italy it had to wait until the 1800s. So it was not a foregone conclusion the central government would prevail.

THE SOLUTION

Edward employed a number of techniques to solve his political and financial problems. Not all of them can be used today exactly the same way Edward used them, but useful lessons can still be learned.

★ War, constant war. It was, for most of Edward's reign, a profitable war for England. It kept potentially troublesome English nobles overseas. Edward instigated a conflict that came to be known as the Hundred Years' War. Actually, it lasted from 1337 to 1453, 116 years of conflict. In the process, Edward further unified England while, ironically, attempting to prevent the French king from doing the same for France. In the 1200s, a series of strong French kings began to strip the English king of his French lands. Soon after Edward III came to throne, a not-so-strong French king sought to complete the process by establishing royal control in the English king's French provinces of Gascony and Guyenne. Edward, rather than simply resisting with military force, upped the ante by claiming the French throne. There was something to Edward's claim, but convincing the French magnates to switch kings would take some doing. England would have to conquer much of France and replace a lot of French magnates. This would take a tremendous effort, as France had over three times the population of England and an even larger GDP. But Edward and his successors kept trying for a century and came close to pulling it off.

The first few years of the war revolved around the English securing their economic interests in Flanders. Once control of Flanders was established, there followed some raids into northern France, but no major battles resulted. Then, in the 1340s, England and France took opposite sides in the long-running civil war over who should be the duke of Brittany. In 1346 this resulted in a

French invasion of Gascony and the shattering French defeat at Crécy. The English then rampaged through western France, until a truce was signed in 1354. The lull in the fighting was brought on by the devastation of the plague, which hit France heavily in 1347–48 and wiped out nearly half of Europe's population in the mid fourteenth century.

The truce didn't last. In 1355, the war began again. In 1356 another major battle was fought at Poitiers, and the French king was captured. English raids continued until 1360, when a peace treaty was signed. Edward agreed to renounce his claim on the French throne in return for the French provinces taken from the English kings in the previous century. Then there was the ransom for the French king, some $300 million of it. The French king died (in 1364) before all the ransom could be collected, and the peace treaty was increasingly ignored by both sides.

Between 1368 and 1396, the French won back much of what the English had taken by adopting "pillage and raid" tactics. At one point, the French even attempted to invade England. Various other campaigns occurred in Spain, Italy, and the Rhineland. During all this, Edward III died in 1377, the year after his heir, the Black Prince, passed away.

Still, for Edward, the war served its purpose, which was to keep his nobles out of mischief in England and make a lot of his subjects rich from French plunder.

★ Leveraged buyout. Edward emulated his ancestor, William of Normandy, and sought to make the war in France pay for itself. At first he tried to pay for military operations out of his income. This did not work. In the first few years of the war, the French played cat and mouse with Edward's army, knowing the English would run out of money to pay their troops. The French were using a much cheaper and less effective feudal levy. So they had plenty of reason to avoid a decisive fight. Edward eventually had to default on over $400 million in loans (mainly from Italian bankers, who found it difficult to badger the king for repayment). Soon Edward realized he had to make the war pay for itself, and this he did by pillaging France and running what amounted to a large-scale protection racket. English nobles and troops became wealthy doing this, and it went on for decades. The French nobles who agreed to ally themselves with the English had their lands left alone. Everyone else in France was fair game, and several generations of English troops went at their work with great gusto and substantial profit. Aside from the pillaging, there were also the sieges and battles. English troops remained superior to the French through most of the war and won most of the battles and sieges. These victories yielded many French nobles as prisoners. The custom of the period was for these prisoners to ransom themselves. These ransoms were negotiated based on the prisoner's rank (knights brought less than counts or kings). A knight or man-at-arms brought $5,000 or more to the captor. This was more than a yeoman made in a year. A lesser noble like a baron could fetch several hundred thousand. Magnates and kings went from a million dollars to, in the case of the French king, $300 million. While there were not many battles, there were hundreds of sieges of castles and walled towns. Here is where the extortion came in. In most cases, the English could be bought off. Or, after they had taken a place, a large payment of cash would get it back into French hands. The payments ranged up to a million dollars or more. Many aristocrats made fortunes during the war, and dozens of castles and mansions built with the loot still stand all over England. The yeomen used their loot to buy more land and improve their farms. For many yeoman families, year after year of successful campaigning enabled them to increase their wealth and landholdings until they were able to buy their way into the minor nobility. Merchants who didn't go to war also did well. Arrows (at a dollar or more each), armor, horses were sold to the troops heading for France, and many returning veterans had jewels, precious metals, and fine cloth they wanted to sell. Several merchants, and a few nobles, acted as bankers, amassing great fortunes in the process. Overall, the English, so to speak, made out like bandits, and Edward had little trouble raising new armies to cross the Channel year after year. In effect, this was a leveraged buyout. Before he died, Edward managed to grab large portions of France while making the French pay for the operation. It was a feat any LBO practitioner would be proud of.

★ Superior military force. The English, with a smaller population, actually had a larger pool of higher-quality troops available than the French. England also had a lock on longbowmen (yeomen), who were also excellent infantry and light cavalry. Thus the English had mobility and quality advantages. For over two centuries, the English had been engaged in constant warfare in Wales, Scotland, and Ireland. As a result of this, they had developed a professional military force using part-time soldiers. Unlike the rest of Europe, where the nobility attempted to monopolize military service, the English had a large number of well-off farmers who were willing to train on their own and serve as longbowmen and light infantry. This training was organized, and the longbowmen were placed in units of a hundred archers. This system took most of the thirteenth century to evolve and only came together in the 1290s. England had very few knights (less than a thousand), but lots of trained commoners who would serve the king for pay and the prospect of pillage. The English troops were disciplined and trained well to do their jobs. This was in sharp contrast to the unruly mobs of feudal warriors commonly found on the Continent.

★ Superior leadership. Many of the English military commanders were excellent. Edward and his son the Black Prince were among the most capable of the medieval generals. The French had to contend with poor generalship. Thus the war started with a larger number of good English commanders, especially commoners who worked their way up. The French looked down on armed commoners. But later on, the French developed some good generals and the English ran out of exceptional commanders. The French also fortified most of central France (at horrendous expense), making it more difficult for the English to live off the land (and provide enough pillage to attract large numbers of those still-superior English men-at-arms and yeomen). The French wore the English down. Sort of like Napoleon or the Germans going into Russia, only in slow motion.

★ Mastery of propaganda. In a period where there were no electronic media, or printing, it was difficult to use modern propaganda techniques. Edward managed to run a masterful public-relations campaign throughout his reign anyway. His main tool was the proclamation. This was a common medieval device, but usually it was a means of proclaiming new laws and regulations. The proclamations were transmitted to the people via public readings at fairs, town squares, and other public functions. Edward used proclamations simply to report on how he was doing in France and in general. The proclamations were purposely written in simple language the common people could understand. Edward reported his successes, his tribulations, and any nasty things the French had said or done. These proclamations, plus the locals going off to fight in France and coming back wealthy, created tremendous enthusiasm for the war. While many of the yeomen going across the Channel didn't come back, or came back crippled and broke, this simply reinforced the idea their king was accomplishing much for England against heavy odds. Medieval life was hard in any event, and the king's French wars enabled a commoner to rise above the rigors of his harsh life.

The historical judgment on Edward has been favorable. But ultimately the war was a disaster for England, leading to the loss of all Continental territories by 1453. However, in Edward's reign the kingdom made a tidy little profit.

The war went on after Edward III's death. After twenty years of skirmishing, in 1397, Charles VI of France and Richard II of England agreed to a thirty-year truce. The English were still in France, the French still wanted the English out, and bands of brigands were rampaging all over the countryside. Civil war was brewing in England and France. Small French forces managed to land in Scotland, England, and Wales to raid and pillage.

In 1413, Henry V (the great grandson of Edward III) came to power in England. Henry allied himself with the Burgundian (dissident members of the French royal family) faction in a French civil war, defeated the French king Charles VI at Agincourt in 1415, and forced a treaty favorable to the English. Henry V's son was declared the heir to the French throne. Charles VI disinherited his own son, the Dauphin, as part of the deal. Henry V married Charles VI's daughter. The son of this marriage (Henry VI) would be the king of France and England. It looked as though England had finally won. But the disinherited Dauphin continued to resist. Henry V unexpectedly died in August 1422, followed in October by Charles VI, with the nine-month-old Henry VI not yet ready to receive the two crowns. Despite the efforts of Henry V's able brothers to hold things together, the Burgundians turned on their English allies, Joan of Arc came and went, and by 1453, the French, aided by these events and the increasing professionalism of their army (they were making extensive use of artillery), had driven the English from the Continent. This gave the English a few years to get ready for their own civil war (the War of the Roses), while the French took care of some internal problems and got ready for the first of many invasions of Italy.

Edward III's legacy was a united England, an England without Continental distractions, and an impressive list of management techniques that can be reused even today.

CHAPTER 7

★ GUSTAVUS ADOLPHUS OF SWEDEN ★

THE ART OF REENGINEERING

GUSTAVUS II, KING of impoverished seventeenth-century Sweden, entered the most destructive war of that century with the apparent odds heavily against him. But Gustavus, like any good manager, had studied the military situation carefully and just as carefully reengineered his army and his country. The results were spectacular, as they would be today for anyone who thought, and acted, as astutely and energetically as Gustavus did.

THE WORLD OF GUSTAVUS ADOLPHUS (1594–1632)

Gustavus came to power in 1611 at the age of seventeen. This "Lion of the North" (as he would later be known) would reign until 1632 (dying in battle). His reign would have a profound effect on European politics and on the way that future wars would be fought.

The Scandinavian countries had been largely ignored since the close of the Viking era (A.D. 800 to 1000). Then, Denmark, Norway, and Sweden fought among themselves for regional domination. From 1389 to 1523, Denmark dominated Sweden and Norway. Denmark's rule began to fall apart in 1512 as the Riksdag, Sweden's national party of burghers, and the peasants lead by Sten Sture, declared Sweden an independent nation. Gustavus Adolphus's grandfather, Gustavus Vasa, finished what Sture had started by expelling Danish forces from Sweden. With Sweden's independence secured, Gustavus Vasa became the king of Sweden. Besides securing Sweden's independence, Gustavus Vasa helped establish Lutheranism in Sweden.

After Gustavus Vasa's death, three of his sons took to the throne one after another. John III, the second to take the throne, strayed somewhat from the Lutheranism his father had supported by marrying Princess Catharine Jagellon of Poland, a staunch Catholic. He unsuccessfully tried to reintroduce Catholicism as the state religion. However, a son resulted from his marriage to Catharine, and this son would be raised a Catholic. John and Catharine's son would be elected to the Polish throne in 1587 as Sigismund III.

John III died in 1594. Because Sigismund III would not accept Lutheranism, Gustavus Vasa's third son, Charles, took advantage of the situation and obtained the throne for himself. As a result of this brotherly conflict, Sweden and Poland would be at odds with each other and would battle on and off into the next century.

Charles began reforming his disorganized government and expanding Sweden's power. He founded the southernmost Swedish town of Göteborg. This gave Sweden clear access to the North Sea and began a war with Denmark in 1611 (the War of Kalmar). While this new war was raging, Charles died. His seventeen-year-old son, Gustavus Adolphus, would pick up where his father left off.

Gustavus Adolphus was born on December 19, 1594. From the start, Gustavus was on the fast track to become ruler of Sweden. His parents, well aware of the burdens their son would have to bear, began his education early. He was educated in the classics, given a strong foundation in Lutheranism, and trained to speak German, Latin, Italian, Russian, and Dutch. Gustavus was the embodiment of the Renaissance man. Charles was forty-three when Gustavus was born, and the average life span for men at the time was not much beyond this. Therefore, Charles wasted no time in involving his son in the ruling of the kingdom. At age nine, Gustavus was taking part in the court of his father. At the ripe age of thirteen, he negotiated officially for his father, and at the age of fifteen he governed a duchy his father had given to him.

When Charles assumed the throne in the place of Sigismund, he had agreed his son would not take the throne until he reached the age of eighteen, and Gustavus would not gain full powers until he was twenty-four. Gustavus was not quite seventeen when his father died. The Riksdag (parliament) saw this as an opportunity to right some injustices that had occurred during the reign of Charles, his brothers, and their father. Thus, there was a power struggle between Gustavus and the Riksdag just as his reign was beginning. In order to resolve the crisis, Gustavus accepted the demands that the Riksdag be more involved in the governing of the state.

One of those drafting the charter Gustavus accepted was Axel Oxenstierna, a twenty-eight-year-old noble who was very talented at government administration. Shortly after Gustavus ascended to the throne, he appointed Oxenstierna as chancellor. This pleased the Riksdag immensely, and it began the formation of a team that would be almost unstoppable.

Once Gustavus dealt with the accession crisis, he turned to the unfinished business of the War of Kalmar. Gustavus fought several border skirmishes with the Danish army, but none of them were conclusive. In the fall of 1612, the English king James I offered to mediate the war between the two northern countries. Both Gustavus and Christian IV, king of Denmark, jumped at the chance to bring the war to a peaceful conclusion. In the negotiated peace, Gustavus kept some of the territory his father had captured from the Danes. But it was kept at a price. Sweden would have to pay Denmark a large sum of money, one million riksdaler, in four installments. Gustavus felt it was worth it to end the war. The official end to the war came on January 28, 1613.

With the War of Kalmar over, Gustavus turned his attention to Russia, where Sweden had been involved in local politics for a long time. The city of Novgorod was in Swedish hands, and Sweden controlled Finland, which bordered Russia. Charles also tried to make one of his younger sons the heir to the Russian throne. In 1615 Gustavus invaded Russia. Several skirmishes and sieges took place over the next couple of years, but nothing dramatic. In February of 1617, Gustavus negotiated a treaty with Russia on terms favorable to Sweden. Russia and Sweden were able to come to terms so quickly because they both felt threatened by Poland.

Poland was still ruled by Gustavus's uncle Sigismund, who still had his eye set on the Swedish throne, and Gustavus saw him as a threat to Sweden and to the Protestant religion. Between 1617 and 1625, Poland and Sweden fought a series of wars. Sweden came out on top, and Gustavus firmly established a Swedish foothold in the eastern Baltic Sea.

At the conclusion of the Polish wars Gustavus turned his attention to a war that had started twelve years earlier, the Thirty Years' War. This conflict was a struggle between the Protestant and Catholic nobles of the Holy Roman Empire. Tensions between the two groups had steadily increased as Protestantism spread throughout Europe. Attempts at a political solution failed. Eventually tensions erupted into an all-out war as the Holy Roman Emperor, Ferdinand II, a Catholic, tried to establish firm control over Protestant German aristocrats. The war raged back and forth across the German states for twelve years before Gustavus became involved in 1630.

Gustavus feared the emperor would gain control of the German states on the Baltic and use them as a launching point to attack Protestant Sweden. For the next two years Gustavus battled side by side with the Protestant German nobles. His two largest victories would be at Breitenfeld and Lützen. Breitenfeld resulted in the loss of thirteen thousand men out of thirty-thousand of the emperor's army, led by Count Tilly. The emperor's force would never fully recover from this loss. At Lützen, Gustavus defeated yet another leading Catholic general, Count Wallenstein. Gustavus's army again devastated the Catholic forces, but Gustavus lost his own life during the fighting. Because of Gustavus's victories Sweden would dominate the Baltic for more than fifty years and the Holy Roman Empire would never be able to rid themselves of their Protestant nobles.

THE CHALLENGE

Sweden in the 1600s, as today, was a small (1.5 million people) up against much larger neighbors. To the immediate south was Denmark (eight hundred thousand people), Sweden's traditional rival. Across the Baltic and to the southeast were Poland (six million) and the German states of the Holy Roman Empire (fifteen million). To the east was the emerging power of Russia (fourteen million). All of these were a potential threat to Sweden's independence. Gustavus, in order to survive, would have to create a potent military force and use it with a deft diplomatic touch.

Not only was Sweden small, but it was economically challenged. Denmark and others had dominated the Baltic area, never allowing Sweden to develop fully her economic capability. Sweden was in a difficult situation. In order to develop she had to control the Baltic, but in order to control the Baltic, she needed resources to develop her armed forces. So, the challenge for Gustavus was to use his small armed forces as effectively as possible.

THE SOLUTION

Gustavus developed a number of techniques familiar to modern managers. But at the time, Gustavus was seen as a daring innovator.

★ Mission statement. Gustavus knew exactly what was best for Sweden, and laid down his policy early on. For Sweden to remain independent, it had to dominate the Baltic Sea. If Sweden did not dominate the Baltic, it would be too easy for other countries to launch invasions into Sweden. Also, domination of the Baltic ports would give Sweden income it sorely needed. Thus, Gustavus had a mission statement guiding him in all of his decisions. When he attacked Russia and Poland, it was not solely to conquer them but to gain the territory on the Baltic. When Gustavus entered the Thirty Years' War, again, his main concern was the Baltic, and helping his fellow Protestants was only his secondary concern. Having such a well-defined mission statement helped Gustavus set his priorities and not get sidetracked into dangerous bypaths.

★ Setting priorities and staying focused. Gustavus could have been easily overwhelmed by his problems with Denmark, Russia, and Poland. Many leaders could have been distracted trying to deal with them all at once. Denmark was the first concern and the most immediate threat. Gustavus wisely went after Denmark right away. Even though the money paid to the Danes for the settlement was immense, it gave Gustavus the time to reorganize his country and prepare for his other challenges. Now Gustavus could deal with either Russia or Poland. Realizing that Russia was the more immediate threat, Gustavus turned there. Also, Russia was a much easier foe than Poland. By the time Gustavus turned to Poland he only had one enemy to deal with, and he had become strong enough to deal with the Polish state, which was no pushover in the seventeenth century.

While fighting Poland, Gustavus was asked to become involved with the Thirty Years' War several times. It would have been premature for him to do so while still struggling with Poland. It must have been tempting for him to become involved with the major conflict of the day. But Gustavus kept his priorities straight and maintained his focus, thus allowing him to succeed.

Gustavus has been criticized at times for not more fully exploiting his great victory at Breitenfeld. With the emperor's army devastated, many felt he should have marched on to Vienna, capturing the emperor's seat of power. If Gustavus had been lured by the glamour of taking Vienna, he would have seriously endangered the foothold he had established in the German states. His army would have been separated from its well-established logistic and communication centers. Gustavus knew his priority was to continue to strengthen his position in Germany. He stayed on task and was not distracted.

★ Partnerships. When Gustavus chose Axel Oxenstierna as his chancellor, he established a very profitable partnership. Oxenstierna's temperament was very different from Gustavus's. Oxenstierna was deliberate; Gustavus was dynamic; Oxenstierna was slow to anger; Gustavus could blow up at a moment's notice; Oxenstierna was an implementer; Gustavus was an idea man. Besides complementing Gustavus, Oxenstierna could be trusted. While Gustavus campaigned through Europe, Oxenstierna took care of matters at home. If Gustavus had not had Oxenstierna, it would have been much more difficult for him to undertake the military campaigns he did. Governing in the seventeenth century was a full-time job, as was leading armies. This partnership allowed Gustavus to do what he was very good at.

Gustavus gave Oxenstierna full authority to do what he thought best. While Gustavus concentrated on building a modern military force, Oxenstierna reformed the Swedish government. With his government reforms, Oxenstierna built a strong home base from which Gustavus drew his strength. Without Oxenstierna, there would have been no Lion of the North.

★ Creative financing. Gustavus looked for a number of ways to finance his military conquests, which were more expensive than Sweden could afford. The first innovation was to reform how his army was paid, which resulted in one of the first truly professional standing armies in Europe. Typically, a soldier did not stay with the army all the time. Therefore, most armies of the day were semiprofessionals. Expensive mercenaries, as well as most officers, were the only full-time professionals. Gustavus came up with a way his troops would stay attached to his army long-term, thus providing a larger number of highly capable professional soldiers. In lieu of taxes, landowners took soldiers onto their farms and provided land, food, and clothing for them. This allowed a soldier to be supported directly, rather than through taxes, and in his off times (when he was not campaigning or training) he would help the landowner with the chores. This was a very efficient way of supporting the troops. This method gave the soldiers a stake in the well-being of the country, thus motivating them to fight harder.

Gustavus also tried many schemes to raise money, none of them very effective. Mostly he had to rely on loans from other countries. In the end, though, he found a solution. His army began to pay for itself in the Thirty Years' War by running what amounted to a protection racket. He found the German states willing to subsidize him after his successes, in order to keep the other armies from returning to pillage their territory. So, by the time Gustavus died, Sweden was on her way to economic prosperity.

★ Leading by example. The only other leader rivaling Gustavus in "leading by example" was Alexander. Often during battle, Gustavus was the first into the fray. As a result he was wounded several times. But it was not only during the heat of battle that he led by example. When Gustavus's army was building fortifications, Gustavus himself would pick up a spade and join the men in digging the trenches. He was killed in Lützen while leading his right-wing cavalry into the thick of battle. Gustavus knew the best way to motivate his men was literally to be up front with them where the action was hottest. He also knew a highly motivated force could overcome a much larger force, and more could be asked of them if he was asking more from himself.

★ Hiring experts. Gustavus recognized innovation when he saw it and borrowed it when he could. For example, at the end of the sixteenth century, the Dutch armies led by Maurice of Nassau gained the Netherlands (Holland) independence from Spain. Maurice developed several innovations in organization and tactics. Gustavus had noticed the Dutch success and began to study Dutch tactics. In addition to studying what Maurice had done, Gustavus went out of his way to hire officers and men who had served in the Dutch forces. Thus he was certain to have people who understood by experience the tactics and innovations of Maurice.

Gustavus also hired many men of science to travel with his army. He had highly qualified engineers to direct the construction of bridges and fortifications. He also had a special corps of miners. He used these experts to train his entire army in the art of fortification and bridging.

★ Hiring the best. During his wars Gustavus tried to use mercenaries as little as possible. There were two reasons for this. First, it was just too expensive to hire mercenaries. Sweden simply could not afford them. A single mercenary regiment, around fifteen hundred men, could cost nearly a million riksdaler a year. Considering Sweden's budget for a year was twelve million riksdaler, this was an enormous cost. Second, they were not as disciplined as his own men and were not trained like his Swedes.

With Sweden's entry into the Thirty Years' War Gustavus was forced to hire mercenaries in order to have a large enough army to oppose the emperor. By Lützen, almost 90 percent of his army were mercenaries. Gustavus was careful to hire mercenaries who would fight within his radically new military system. Many mercenaries were too independent and would not follow orders or conform to their employer's military systems. Gustavus was particularly fond of Scottish units and went out of his way to employ them. The Dutch were another source of soldiers who fought well for Gustavus. By picking and choosing his mercenaries, and not just hiring bodies, Gustavus used them effectively in his campaigns.

★ Communication. Gustavus had to communicate at many different levels. First, he had to communicate his political intentions to the Riksdag back in Sweden. Second, he had to communicate his plans for battle to his officers. Third, he had to communicate his values and principles to his troops. He was an expert at all of these. Some of the speeches he gave to the Riksdag rank with the best of Swedish literature. Gustavus had to make sure that when he stood in front of the Riksdag, he effectively addressed the concerns of his subjects' representatives. In addition, he had to ask for commitments from them. He did this by reminding them of their responsibilities, and then motivating them by letting them know that if Sweden became great, they each would, also, become great. Gustavus was considered to be one of the greatest orators of his day.

On the battlefield he made sure each unit understood what its objectives were. He would ride from unit to unit before a battle giving each individual instructions. His orders left no doubt what he expected from his soldiers and the fact that the boss personally delivered those orders did wonders for the soldiers' morale.

Gustavus lived his religion and wanted his troops to do the same. He communicated this desire through written means and by his official actions as army commander. In 1621, he issued a set of field regulations covering all areas of a soldier's life. It detailed how soldiers were supposed to act and the punishments for those who violated the regulations. Gustavus wanted a truly Christian army. Thus, there were punishments for looting and rape, besides the more usual punishments for violation of army discipline. Gustavus's army was the least brutal, to the general population, of any during the Thirty Years' War. Also, Gustavus discouraged camp followers (usually female, to take care of housekeeping and sexual needs of the troops). Another way he communicated his religious intents was to have morning and evening prayer. Everyone in the army participated in these prayers. There was no doubt among Gustavus's soldiers as to his religious principles.

★ Reengineering. Gustavus radically changed the way war was fought in his day. This was one of his best remembered achievements. By reengineering his armed forces, he created an army nearly unbeatable by older-style forces. His reengineering effort consisted of recognizing a change was needed; making radical changes; and using technology in new ways to support the changes he was making. Because of the changes he implemented, he is considered the father of modern warfare.

Gunpowder weapons had been in use since the fourteenth century, but battlefield tactics had not changed much at all. Troops would still line up in large formations of densely packed men. A typical unit with some sixteen hundred men would have a frontage of about a hundred yards. This meant twenty to forty rows of men deep, usually translating to a unit depth of twenty-five to fifty yards. These large units would consist of two types of troops. First, on the flanks would be men armed with muskets, which could hit horses and riders a hundred meters away. Behind the musketeers were pikemen. The pikes were twelve-to-sixteen-foot-long spears for warding off enemy cavalry attacks while the musketeers reloaded, or the entire formation was moving. This formation also worked against infantry, although similar musket/pike units would slowly chop each other to pieces with musket fire and "push of pike." The problem was that the men were packed so densely that only the first few rows could actually participate in the battle. Maurice of Nassau, the Dutch general mentioned earlier, had recognized that if he could reduce the number of rows, he would extend the length of his line and bring more firepower to bear on the enemy. Maurice also reduced the size of his units in battle and created more of them. This made it easier to move troops around the battlefield and form them up effectively for combat.

Gustavus recognized that the changes Maurice had made were significant and, if applied correctly, could allow a smaller force to defeat a larger force still using the old style of organization. Maurice might have started the revolution in tactics, but Gustavus perfected it. Gustavus further reduced the size of individual units on the battlefield. This allowed his forces to be still more mobile in battle.

Another change Gustavus made was to have his muskets fire in a salvo rather than the more cumbersome method currently in use. The older practice was for the first row of muskets to fire and then move behind the rows of musketeers to the rear, to reload while the next row fired. This produced a constant stream of fire. But it did not produce an enormous amount of firepower. Gustavus lined up his troops so three rows could fire simultaneously. This amount of firepower was devastating to enemy formations. To further exploit this, Gustavus turned his pikemen from musketeer bodyguards into attackers. Pikemen were normally used to defend the musketeers while they reloaded. Gustavus saw the chance to use them to rush into the enemy formations devastated and disorganized by the musket volley. To facilitate this, he shortened the pike and reinforced its shaft near the spear tip so it could not be chopped off during battle. The shorter pike was also easier to handle in a pitched battle.

Gustavus also changed the way cavalry was used. With the widespread use of muskets and pikes, the cavalry could no longer boldly charge into masses of infantry. For a thousand years, that tactic had worked to break up infantry formations. Cavalry now hung on the edges of the battlefield, threatening and harassing the enemy where they could. Typically, the cavalry would ride close to the infantry, fire their pistols or muskets, then wheel away to retreat and reload. This was not very effective. Gustavus's new infantry tactics gave the cavalry the opportunity to become effective again. The cavalry now looked for opportunities to exploit the devastation caused by the mass fire of the infantry. Coordinating their efforts with the infantry, they would charge into recently shot-up enemy units. They would still fire their pistols or muskets. But now, instead of wheeling, they would draw swords and attack the front lines of the enemy infantry. This was effective because the musket fire had broken down the wall of pikes. It was a prime example of old technology being revived by the use of new technology.

Artillery became more effective under Gustavus. The first change he made was to standardize on only three calibers of artillery guns. This made it easier to supply the battlefield with ammunition. Also, one of the artillery types was the light three-pounder, which became known as the regimental gun. These light guns could now, for the first time, be moved quickly around the battlefield to where they were needed. Innovations were made so the powder and the shot were packaged together with a wire cage. This allowed the regimental guns actually to reload and fire faster than the muskets. Gustavus's changes to his artillery system proved devastating to the enemy. Artillery was capable of delivering the most concentrated and damaging firepower, and the Swedish guns were the best organized and efficient. If the Swedes got their guns into action during a battle, the enemy was in big trouble.

Gustavus made numerous other changes. He modified the muskets so they were lighter and more reliable, a very popular move with the troops. He changed the way in which soldiers were recruited and paid in Sweden. He changed the method by which his armies were supplied. And there are many other minor and major changes he carried out. An entire book could probably be written on his reengineering efforts. Gustavus continually looked for ways to improve his country and his army, and he was not afraid to make radical changes. One key to Gustavus's success was that he made changes at the appropriate times. His father had tried to make some of the same changes, but made the mistake of doing it while his army was distracted by the war with Poland. The results were disastrous. Gustavus learned from this mistake and made his changes at times when he could spend the time to retrain his army.

If Gustavus had lived past his fortieth birthday, it would have been interesting to see what impact he would have continued to have on warfare and on Europe. By keeping his priorities straight, by keeping focused, and by embracing radical change, he achieved more in a few years than most men do in an entire lifetime.

CHAPTER 8

★ FREDERICK THE GREAT OF PRUSSIA ★

CALCULATED LEVERAGE

A GENERATION BEFORE the American Revolution, Frederick the Great, the king of Prussia, lost as many battles as he won, but always did so with far fewer resources than his opponents. Descended from a line of frugal and calculating kings, Frederick entered the high-stakes game of war and international politics with the deck heavily stacked against him. Yet Frederick prevailed, and not because of luck or divine intervention. The lessons he learned, applied, and built upon are still valid.

Frederick was known as the Great not because he conquered Europe, or even large parts of it. He was known as the Great because he was able to survive while surrounded by more powerful enemies. Had Frederick not been around, Prussia would likely have been absorbed by one or more of its larger neighbors. This is what happened to Poland and several smaller nations at that time. Frederick was able to take what few resources he had and leverage them in order to prosper in the cauldron of European politics. Frederick's reign is the example which all small businesses can build upon when they find themselves surrounded by rapacious giants.

THE WORLD OF FREDERICK THE GREAT (1712–1786)

Germany was the muddle in the middle of the European powers of the eighteenth century. What we today know as Germany was a collection of over a hundred small principalities that owed their allegiance to the figurehead Holy Roman Empire. As the other European powers had congealed and grown into nations, the Germans had remained a collection of independent feudal states. To make matters worse, the Thirty Years' War (1618–1648) had been fought largely on German soil, leaving the area devastated, depopulated, and feeling the aftereffects for several centuries thereafter.

The 1648 Treaty of Westphalia finally brought peace to northern Europe. One of the principalities to emerge from this settlement was Brandenburg (the area around Berlin), ruled by the Elector William Frederick, the great-grandfather of Frederick the Great. An elector was one of the handful of German rulers voting for the Holy Roman Emperor each time an incumbent died. William Frederick also ruled over Prussia to the east. William Frederick ended his reign known as the Great Elector because of his revitalization of Brandenburg-Prussia as a regional power.

William Frederick was succeeded by his son. Because of his support of the Holy Roman Emperor in several wars, the son was allowed to use the title king and thus became Frederick I, king of Prussia. Frederick I also ran up an enormous debt his son would have to deal with. Frederick I styled himself as a French king and tried to live as one.

Frederick I died in 1713 and his son Frederick William I succeeded him. Frederick II (soon to be the Great) was the one-year-old heir to his father's new throne. Frederick I had expanded the Prussian territory through peaceful means. He had also continued to strengthen his army, but he left his son with a lot of debts. Frederick William I despised the French lifestyle his father had loved so much and saw anything French as a weakness. He also had a financial crisis caused by his father's free spending on his hands.

The first thing the new Prussian king did was to dismantle the French-style court system his father had built. The new king lived more like a bürgermeister (town mayor) than a monarch. French ways were shunned, although ironically French remained the language of the Prussian nobles. Frederick William I continued to build the army of his father and grandfather. He dedicated as much as 80 percent of his annual revenue to military matters.

Frederick William I was married to Sophia Dorothea, the daughter of the Elector of Hanover. This was the same Elector of Hanover soon to become King George I of England. This fact would have a great effect on Frederick the Great, as England would be involved in German politics throughout Frederick's life. Having England as an ally proved to be a considerable asset.

Under Frederick William I, the army continued to grow. By the time of his death, the standing army numbered eighty-three thousand, the fourth largest army in Europe. This was an outstanding achievement considering that the population of Prussia was less than three million.

The Prussian soldiers were not all Prussian subjects. In fact, Frederick William I used foreign recruits as much as possible. This brought him much praise as being an "enlightened ruler" because he did not always subject his own people to the horrors of military service.

Frederick William was an eccentric. He had one regiment composed of soldiers all six feet or taller. He had a number of other eccentricities and a terrible temper. Speculation is he had the same mental affliction King George III suffered from. This condition would cause him to act irrationally at times. Because of this, Frederick the Great and Frederick William I had a very volatile relationship. Frederick the Great was nearly strangled to death by his father when he and a friend were caught trying to escape from Prussia. Throughout his teenage years, Frederick was often beaten with the cane his father always carried.

Frederick William I raised his son with a lot of strict discipline, adding to the strained relationship. Young Frederick was never left alone. A tutor or servant was always watching over him. This was done, supposedly, to keep young Frederick from indulging in carnal temptations. Each day Frederick had a strict schedule of religious services and training activities. He was not allowed to study anything French, although, paradoxically, all his training was done in French. Frederick never learned to read or speak German well and was permitted no Latin training because of its connection with the Catholic Church. It is perhaps this strict upbringing that would make Frederick the disciplined leader he would later become.

The relationship between Frederick William I and "young Fritz" was so strained the two of them spent little time with each other. Shortly before Frederick William I died, the two were somewhat reconciled. In his later life, Frederick always gave credit to his father for laying the foundation for his success.

By the time Frederick William I died in 1740, he had restored his kingdom's finances through his austere ways. He had expanded the borders of Prussia to include a port on the Baltic. And he left his son an army second to none in quality.

Frederick would put the army to good use. Shortly after his accession to the throne, Frederick would expand his borders by invading neighboring Silesia. Later Frederick would use the same army to keep Silesia and to survive the Seven Years' War (1756–63) which was mainly about the attempted destruction of Prussia by the Austrian Empire and her allies.

THE CHALLENGE

When Frederick took the throne of Prussia in 1740, he entered a world awash in political intrigue. Prussia was surrounded by potential enemies. To the east was Russia, to the south were the Austrians and the Holy Roman Empire, to the west were the French. There were also the British, the Swedes, and the other German principalities to worry about. Any of these potential adversaries outnumbered the Prussians from two to five times, and when allied together they were overwhelming. Frederick's first challenge was survival.

Survival was not enough for the new king. By making strong alliances with either the French or the British, Frederick could have ensured his survival by giving up independence or territory. Giving up territory was not an option, as Prussia was already too small. Giving up any sliver of independence was intolerable for the strong-willed Prussians. The ambitious new Prussian king saw survival achieved by expanding his small kingdom. He would always have to defeat larger armies and would need to avoid upsetting all his neighbors at once.

Another challenge Frederick imposed on himself was that of being an "enlightened prince." This was a humanist philosophy his grandfather had practiced. A key aspect of this was the concept that a monarch served his subjects. Frederick had also acquainted himself with writings of the current "Age of Reason," the same ideas that brought about the American Revolution and the founding of the United States.

The great French philosopher Voltaire was a friend of Frederick. Voltaire, the theoretical fellow, eventually quarreled a lot with Frederick, the practical king. This led Frederick to quip—"If I wanted to punish a province, I would put a philosopher in charge."

Frederick even wrote a book titled the *Anti-Machiavel,* wherein he described how the "enlightened prince" should act. This book was published shortly before he ascended to the throne. Frederick would struggle with the ideals of this book and the realities of politics of the time.

Frederick's career was thus filled with political and military crises, plus his self-imposed obligation to rule his kingdom in an enlightened way. Oh, and Frederick was also an accomplished musician and composer. His musical compositions have stood the test of time and are still performed.

THE SOLUTION

Fortunately for Frederick, he had a wealth of talents and techniques available to meet the challenges he faced throughout his career.

★ Recognizing opportunity. Frederick knew an opportunity when he saw it and rarely let one go by unused. Shortly after Frederick became king, the Holy Roman Emperor died. There were no male heirs, only a strong-willed daughter, Maria Theresa. The daughter wanted the throne for herself, but the Electors of the Holy Roman Empire believed strongly in Salic Law (inheritance can only be passed from father to son). Having no clear successor to the throne caused an uproar among the Holy Roman Electors. To complicate matters, the other major European nations were distracted. France and England were busy fighting each other, and Russia had just lost its empress. The Austrian and Hungarian armies Maria Theresa commanded were in poor condition from recent battles with the Turks. This had also left Maria Theresa's treasury empty. With the Austrians weak, without an emperor, and all the other interested parties distracted, Frederick saw an opportunity to expand Prussia. Frederick felt that in the political confusion it would be possible to seize the Austrian province of Silesia, which bordered Brandenburg. With a population of 1.5 million industrious Poles and Germans, it would be a nice addition to the Prussian kingdom.

Once having recognized the opportunity, Frederick was faced with the challenge of the "enlightened prince," who could not just bully his way through the world taking what he wanted. There had to be a justification for taking Silesia. Brandenburg had a historical claim to Silesia, even if it was somewhat dubious. Because of this claim, Frederick could justify the invasion to himself on the principle that an "enlightened prince" must always defend the state and keep the state's interest at heart. If Frederick did not pursue the claim on Silesia, the state's interest and its security would be at risk. Whether the young king was justified or not, Silesia did become part of the Prussian state because Frederick was able to recognize the opportunity and did not fail to pursue it. Frederick saw many other opportunities during his reign, and managed to make something of every one of them.

★ Personal leadership and respect for subordinates. Frederick the Great's troops were always highly motivated. This was accomplished through several techniques, but mostly through Frederick's own personal leadership. Frederick lived in a time where the role of statesman and general were beginning to split. The French king did not lead his troops into battle; neither did the English king. But Frederick shared the battlefield with his men. He shared the same food and living conditions. He also was very familiar with his troops. He would laugh and joke with them. During campaigns he was always among the common soldiers, encouraging them to keep going. Frederick's attitude about the common man must have shown through to his troops. Frederick really believed all men were equal. He wrote about this several times in his books. Some have felt he did not value his troops' lives. Indeed he did, but he felt both the commoner and the king were subservient to the fatherland and, if necessary, must die for the common good. The commoner and the noble each had their role, but in the end they were equal.

Frederick did not take himself too seriously, either. A story told of him in his later years illustrates this point. Frederick was out riding one day when he found a laughing crowd gathered before a poster. As he got closer he could see it was an unflattering caricature of him. Instead of having it ripped down, he noticed it had been placed a bit too high to see. He had an assistant lower it, much to the amusement of his subjects. Another part of Frederick's personal leadership style was his ability to share the credit for his victories. Wherever possible he gave credit to the men he led. He showed considerable respect to his officers and men, and this was reciprocated.

★ Mentors and personal training. Because of his father, Frederick's early education was incomplete. Once Frederick was free of his father, he filled in the gaps. Before ascending the throne, and when he was living apart from his father, he studied as much as he could. He would study from 4 A.M. until noon. After taking care of business in the afternoon, he hit the books again into the night. He slowly made up for his inadequate education as a child. He continued to educate himself throughout his life. Besides study, Frederick surrounded himself with men of learning and great talent. Throughout his life, he maintained a relationship with the great French thinker Voltaire. He also sought out men of learning from around Prussia and Europe and convinced them to become part of his court. Frederick's reputation as an intellectual, plus the usual monetary blandishments, brought the great minds of the eighteenth century flocking to Prussia. In the military area, he had his grandfather's and father's best general to tutor him, Prince Leopold I, the Old Dessauer. Frederick used this great military master as his mentor for as long as both were alive. Both on and off the battlefield, Frederick sought to improve his capabilities and surround himself with great talent to do it. He succeeded.

★ Finding good men and keeping them. Frederick knew that in order to win the battles, he would need the best officer corps possible. He followed the tradition of his father and grandfather of using Prussian aristocrats as officers. He also cast about for talented foreign professionals. One way he got officers of the highest quality was to offer twice the money any other kingdom was paying. The high quality of Frederick's army also attracted many of the best officers from the surrounding states. In order to keep these men of quality, Frederick would promote them as fast possible when they were successful. He also at times used cash grants to reward his successful leaders.

★ Leisure. Frederick understood the importance of leisure. If a leader is always working, he would burn out or, at the very least, become a sour fellow. Frederick's three main leisurely activities were playing the flute, composing music, and writing verse. He would share these pursuits with his officers in the evenings. It must have made him seem more human to them. Then again, maybe not. Sitting there listening to one's king perform music he himself had composed must have been impressive, if not a bit intimidating. Another benefit of these hobbies was that they helped him relax. He would read poetry the night before battle in order to help him think. It apparently worked, for Frederick was known to be always clear-headed and unflappable. He also wrote books and engaged in lively discussions, debates, and sometimes outright arguments with the artists and scientists he attracted to his court.

★ Learning from mistakes. From the start of his military career, Frederick analyzed his battles and looked for ways to improve his army and battlefield technique. During his was for Silesia, after his first battle with the Austrians, Frederick produced a brutally honest tactical summary and left no excuses for himself, or anyone else. He would continue to follow this example throughout his career. In the campaigns of 1743, Frederick discovered that his cavalry commanders were not taking advantage of opportunities because of a lack of orders. Frederick thereafter encouraged the cavalry to attack without orders. In fact, he threatened to sack commanders who allowed themselves to be attacked first.

★ Training. The Prussian army had a century-old tradition of intense training. Frederick's army relentlessly drilled and maneuvered when they were not campaigning. To defeat his more numerous opponents, the Prussians had to be able to react faster and perform all maneuvers to perfection. One way to get them to react faster was to march them quickly from one place to another. The Prussians perfected the art of marching, and Frederick built upon it. The training Frederick put his troops through was not easy. At times it collided with his "enlightened prince" self. For example, Frederick noticed several members of his cavalry had been maimed or died during training. When he brought this to the attention of his cavalry commanders, the response was, "If you make a fuss about a few broken necks, Your Majesty, you will never have the bold horsemen you require for the field." The tough training continued. Besides maneuvers Frederick instructed his officers in the theory of war. After the war for Silesia, Frederick wrote instruction manuals for infantry and cavalry operations. These were regarded as state secrets, for they contained the battlefield wisdom of the great Frederick. He wrote a second treatise called *General Principles of War*. He also wrote about leading a state, and in circulating these writings Frederick, in effect, trained his senior commanders.

★ Outsourcing. In order to have the large standing army he needed, Frederick, like his father, had to rely on mercenaries. If he had limited himself to Prussians, he would have devastated his own economy. He simply did not have the people to maintain an army of the size needed to compete against Prussia's neighbors. At the start of the Seven Years' War (1756–1763), nearly a third of his forces were foreigners. This ratio would remain fairly constant throughout the war. Frederick would have liked to use more foreigners, thus risking fewer of his countrymen, but he was never able to find as many mercenaries as he would have liked even though he had recruiting agents in almost every European country. With every country looking to fill the ranks of its army, and standing armies coming into vogue, there were just not enough men to go around. Frederick tried to overcome this by paying more than other countries and even impressing into service those captured in battle.

★ Innovation. The greatest challenge Frederick faced on the battlefield was that his forces were almost always outnumbered. Intensive training and the quality of his officers helped offset his numerical inferiority somewhat. But what really won battles for Frederick was his innovative tactics. Frederick was not the prolific innovator Gustavus was, but his changes were significant. Frederick noted reloading muskets faster made it possible to reduce the number of ranks in the battle line. During the sixteenth and seventeenth centuries, the lines had been five or six men deep because of the slow speed of reloading. By Frederick's time, the line had thinned to three rows. This meant, for the same number of men, the line of battle could be longer. Typically the army with the longest line was more likely to outflank its opponent and win the battle. If the army was always the smallest force on the field, it was always in danger of being outflanked. Frederick's use of thinner lines of better-drilled (and faster-firing) musketeers enabled him successfully to face larger armies. Frederick also capitalized on his better-trained troops to develop a devastating new tactic—the oblique order. This maneuver worked by having one portion of the army remain in front of the enemy. The other portion of the army would march in columns, one staggered behind the other in an echelon formation, at an oblique angle to the enemy. Each of these columns would eventually reach the flank of the enemy and, one after the other, would crash into the flank somewhat farther down from the first-arriving column. The attacking force would be supported by all available cavalry and artillery. The idea was to crush one side of the enemy's battle line and then roll up the flank of the remaining portion of the line. Some very fancy marching was needed to pull off this complicated maneuver. Frederick's superior training of his men made this tactic work and pay off for him again and again.

Another tactical innovation of Frederick's was horse artillery. Frederick noticed that many of his cavalry and fast-marching infantry were left unsupported by the artillery. At the time, artillery was slowly dragged about the battlefield by large horses. Frederick developed horse-drawn light artillery groups that could be moved quickly around the battlefield. Until this time the artillery was drawn by horse, but the men who loaded and fired the guns walked. Frederick had all artillerymen on horseback. Now artillery could move with the cavalry and be brought up rapidly to support the infantry.

★ Persistence. During the Seven Years' War Frederick lost battles as often as he won them. Any other leader would have given up, but after a defeat he would rebuild his forces and face his enemy again and again. Eventually, this tenacity paid off and the alliance formed against him fell apart in 1762 with the death of the Russian czar. The new czar, Peter III, was a big fan of Frederick and quickly joined forces with the Prussian king. After that Frederick was never again seriously threatened.

Frederick left a legacy that still influences Germany. The Germans used the lessons and military traditions Frederick left them to build a nation that became a leading economic and military power by the end of the nineteenth century. But first, Frederick delivered one final lesson, twenty years after he died. In 1806 the French army blew the Prussians off the battlefield at Jena. This was, well, shocking. What happened to the army of Frederick the Great? It was simple. Without Frederick and his inspired leadership, there was no army of Frederick. In the two decades after Frederick, those he left behind missed what made Frederick special. Many of Frederick's habits were dismissed as eccentric and not important. What was kept was the iron discipline and careful attention to the finer points of marching in a straight line. The French, under Napoleon and his able marshals, were thinking like Frederick while the Prussians were trying to act like Frederick. Big difference; and the French had it right. Seven years later, the Prussians had recovered and eventually won their last battle with the French at Waterloo in 1815. In the decades after Waterloo, the Prussian army finally absorbed the lessons of Frederick. Thus, well into the twentieth century, the German army was the most formidable on the planet. Fortunately, Frederick's strategic genius was not captured. The German army in the twentieth century could win many battles, but always lost its wars. In the end, Frederick's successors were only able to recover half of their inheritance.

CHAPTER 9

★ NAPOLEON OF FRANCE ★
THE MANAGER OF REVOLUTION

NAPOLEON WAS THE master of the battlefield, but he was also the master of management in general and government organization and administration in particular. France, and many other nations, still live with the wide-ranging reforms Napoleon instituted when he basically took over the French Revolution and turned it into a tool for reshaping every aspect of French officialdom. The government of France, and the rest of Europe, has never been the same since.

THE WORLD OF NAPOLEON (1769–1821)

It was, so to speak, the best of times and the worst of times. Napoleon Bonaparte was born on Corsica in 1769, the son of a leader in the Corsican resistance to French rule. A year after Napoleon's birth, his father, and the rest of the resistance movement, admitted defeat and, as part of the deal, his father was admitted to the French nobility. This enabled Napoleon to enter a French army school in 1779 as a nine-year-old cadet. Five years later he entered officer school and in 1785 received a commission in the French army. This got him started on his career of conquest. During his education, an aptitude for mathematics was noted, as well as an enthusiasm for military life in general.

The officers' school Napoleon attended, founded in 1751 to instill some professional competence in the largely aristocratic (and lackadaisical) officers' corps, normally took two or three years of study. But Napoleon hastened through it in one year. His instructors noted Napoleon was something special. Napoleon was sent to an artillery regiment, where there was always a need for bright and technically competent officers.

Meanwhile, revolution was in the air. The Corsicans were not the only French subjects willing to fight for freedom. As a teenager, Napoleon heard all about the American Revolution, and this event inspired many of his generation. The French Revolution began in 1789, which found Napoleon in a very fortunate position. He was a junior army officer (four years' service), thus less threatened by the purges of officers that took place in the next few years. While he was a member of the nobility, his father was a known Corsican rebel, and this provided additional protection. Best of all, nearly half of the army officers fled the country once the revolution had taken control of the government. This provided ample promotion opportunities for those officers who stayed.

The political problems in France stemmed from the economic success of the country. Like other European nations, France was still ruled, and largely owned, by the less than 2 percent of the population comprising the ancient feudal aristocracy. For several centuries, a middle class (merchants, professionals, manufacturers, etc.) had been gaining control over a larger portion of the French economy. The farmers, who still comprised the majority of the population, at least got something back from the middle class when they did business with them. Not so with the feudal aristocrats, who continued to collect taxes and free labor as they had for over a thousand years. The American Revolution had given people an example of how one could be free of ancient oppression. Moreover, France had been poorly governed in the late 1700s, and a major crop failure in 1788 had created a financial crisis in the government and riots in the streets. The king needed more money and peace. The middle class was the most likely source of cash and calm. But simply to ask these people for anything would be politically risky, so the king called the Estates-General in 1789. This French "parliament" had last met in 1614, and by calling it the king unleashed a force he could not control.

Three "estates" were represented in the Estates-General: the nobility, the clergy, and the commoners. The wealthy and highly educated commoners soon took over, for the "Third Estate" represented some 90 percent of the population and the summer of 1789 was the season of revolution. The king gave in, bit by bit, and by the end of the year the new democratically elected National Constituent Assembly abolished most of the ancient privileges. The First Republic was declared on September 22, 1792. This aroused all the royalists in neighboring countries, especially Austria and Prussia. By the end of 1793, the new French republic was at war with most European monarchies. The French king tried to leave the country, was caught, and tried for treason. King Louis XVI was beheaded on January 21, 1793. His wife, Queen Marie Antoinette, was beheaded on October 16, 1793.

The wars did not go well, and royalists in various parts of France violently resisted the new republican government. The French government reacted to all these troubles with the Reign of Terror during which tens of thousands of opponents (real or imagined) of the revolution were executed. Soon the desperate revolutionary rulers of France turned on each other. Between late 1793 and 1795 power shifted from the radicals to moderates, the latter of whom paid more attention to military matters and making the new government work.

Napoleon was only twenty when the revolution really got going in 1789. He got in trouble early on for getting sidetracked with Corsican politics and not having the right political mentors. But he was able to maintain his position as a French army officer and worked his way up to general's rank. In 1796 he led an army to defeat Austrian and Italian armies in Italy and eliminated any threat to France's southeastern borders. This gained him great prestige with the French government, and he was able to talk the ruling council into giving him an army and fleet with which to invade Egypt as a first step toward taking India away from England. In 1798 Napoleon defeated Egyptian forces and captured Alexandria, the largest city in Egypt. The British, however, destroyed the French fleet, thus cutting Napoleon's army off from France. Realizing his position was untenable, Napoleon went back to France and did what he had thus far avoided doing, taking over the French government.

Napoleon did not think of himself as a politician, but rather a "man of action." While he had been out winning battles for France, the French revolutionary government had been sinking into corruption and ineffectiveness. Napoleon had been building up his political power over the years, but always as a secondary task in support of his battlefield activities. But now, with his Egyptian campaign in a shambles and the situation back in Paris getting more unsteady, Napoleon decided to act.

In 1799 Napoleon became the dictator (first consul) of France. This should have been no surprise. Napoleon had waged an impressive propaganda campaign out front while, behind the scenes, collecting an imposing array of allies within the government. While many opposed this move, Napoleon had most people behind him.

In 1802 Napoleon had himself declared "Consul for life." Same drill as 1799; Napoleon did his homework and lined up all the popular and political support he needed. France was tired of the incompetence and corruption of the revolutionary politicians. General Bonaparte proved as capable at the head of the nation as he had at the head of his army.

Napoleon continued the French program of exporting the revolution to nearby nations. Napoleon also realized a centuries-old French dream of dominating Italy. In 1802 he got himself elected president of the Cisalpine (Northern Italian) Republic. This area had long been a fertile ground for revolutionary ideas, and Napoleon had supported prorevolution and pro-French thinking among the locals during his years of campaigning in Italy. Napoleon was also of Italian extraction, a point not lost on Italians.

At the same time, Napoleon made peace with all of France's enemies, including England and, most importantly, the pope. The French Revolution had been particularly hostile to the Church, as most modern revolutions have been. Napoleon was more realistic and spoke publicly of the need for religion and morality. He befriended clergy and respected religious practices. This caused Napoleon some problems with his own generals and government officials, but he knew the majority of the people were still religious, and his approach would make him appear as the friend of the many citizens who feared the revolution or were still religious. These two groups always comprised the majority of people in Europe, and even in revolutionary France.

In 1804 Napoleon became the French emperor, placing the crown on his own head. He saw himself as the successor of Charlemagne, not the previous French king, Louis XVI. Conspirators against Napoleon, seeking the restoration of Louis XVIII (brother of Louis XVI, Louis XVII had died earlier) to the throne, caused a minor stir. But the French people were more pleased with the issuing of the new civil code, which gave the entire country one set of laws, than they were with Napoleon's coronation.

While France was happy with all this new government, the rest of Europe's aristocrats were still horrified at what the French were up to. Napoleon's return to monarchy was meant to calm the other crowned heads of Europe, but it was no secret Napoleon was also the prime mover behind government reorganizations that eliminated many of the goodies aristocrats had feasted on for centuries. Even Napoleon's new nobility had to settle for grand titles, pensions, some real estate, and many fancy uniforms. None of this being a little king on a noble's estates with the ability to play judge and jury with his subjects. The French people could still vote for some officials, and they knew Napoleon paid close attention to public opinion. Napoleon was one of those rare emperors who acted like he was always running for reelection.

Britain was France's most implacable enemy, and was at war with Napoleon constantly, except for about a year during 1802–3. Britain's superior fleet made this possible, preventing the French from getting their enormous army to Britain. The dispute between Britain and France was more about economics than politics, for Britain was the most liberal and democratic of the European monarchies. Napoleon early on decided the way to defeat Britain was to prevent trade between the Continent and Britain. Didn't work. There were too many ports and eager customers, and not enough French troops to keep all the forbidden goods out.

The Continental System of Napoleon was fine in theory. Mainland Europe could produce all it needed without overseas trade. But many of the goods coming in by ship were in big demand (coffee and sugar, for example), and although Napoleon was able to hurt British trade, he could not stop it. But the damage was also felt by Britain's Continental customers, and this caused growing resentment against the French.

In 1805, Austria and Russia joined with Britain to attack France. Napoleon quickly turned the tables and defeated Russia and Austria at Austerlitz. A few more battles were fought, and that coalition collapsed. The following year, the same coalition tried again, this time with Prussia added. Napoleon defeated them all, and peace was again made in 1807. At this point Napoleon was thirty-eight years old.

But the Continental System proved Napoleon's undoing, with a little help from a six-year guerilla war in Spain, where Napoleon had tried to replace the legitimate king with his brother. The Spanish people noticed and, with help from British troops and supplies, never stopped fighting. Then came disaster in Russia.

The Russian czar eventually renounced support of the Continental System, for Russia desperately needed overseas trade. With Russia opting out, the Continental System would fail, and fail quickly. So Napoleon invaded Russia. Big mistake. He reached and occupied Moscow, but there were not sufficient roads for moving supplies to support an army that large. The troops had to be gotten out of Russia before they starved to death, for the Russians refused to surrender even with many of their major cities occupied. Napoleon took 655,000 troops into Russia. Only about 85,000 came out by the end of the year. Some 370,000 died of illness, exposure, and combat (roughly in that order). Another 200,000 became prisoners, of whom half died. This was a catastrophic loss, even though only about half the troops were actually French. The rest were allies from just about every corner of Europe (except Britain). But even this was a disadvantage, for the survivors of those foreign contingents went home and told everyone the French were not, as they had been until 1812, invincible. The French could be beaten.

The French, despite their popular ideas for liberalizing the feudal state of European politics, placed the interests of France ahead of every other nation's. The Continental System was the most visible example of this. Another was the arrogant conduct of French diplomacy, while Napoleon's unbeaten army stood ready to enforce decisions made in Paris.

After the 1812 campaign, most European nations were swept with a nationalist fervor, a desire to free themselves of French domination and obtain revenge for past military defeats. The monarchs and aristocrats of these nations, particularly the German-speaking ones, promoted these ideas, even though in subsequent decades this nationalism would cause numerous rebellions and social upheavals. But for the moment, many people, commoner and noble, wanted to be free of French authority. Napoleon had shown how a revolution could be tamed and redirected; now other heads of state were aiming their controlled revolutions at France. This became a force even Napoleon's enormous talents could not deal with.

Austria, Prussia, Russia, and many smaller German states defeated French armies in central Europe during 1813 and invaded France in 1814. Napoleon was forced to abdicate and sent into exile. In early 1815 Napoleon returned, and the French people supported him over the restored king, But the armies of Europe again defeated Napoleon and sent him into exile under guard. Napoleon died of cancer in 1821.

THE CHALLENGE

Starting with nothing but a junior officer's commission, Napoleon had to overcome all obstacles to become ruler of France and master of Europe and beyond.

But first, there were life and death matters. Revolutions tend to eat their children, and the French Revolution was no different. After the more rabid revolutionaries had killed each other off in the late 1790s, Napoleon stepped in and picked up the pieces. In 1799, shortly after turning thirty, he participated in a coup to replace the five-man Directory (office of the president) with one-man rule of himself as consul (president of France).

Gaining power, as Napoleon discovered, required rather different skills than those used to keep control of the most powerful nation in Europe. In 1800, France had a population of 22 million, although Napoleon soon added adjacent areas to swell the "French" population to nearly 30 million. Of Napoleon's principal enemies, Great Britain had only 9.5 million people. The Austrian Empire had 24 million people. Prussia had nine million, and what passed for Germany in those days (a collection of independent states) had 24 million. Russia had thirty million people, Spain had 9.5 million, and Portugal 2.8 million. Italy, another collection of independent states, had 15 million people. What Napoleon had to do was make France strong enough to deal with the military might of more populous coalitions. Most of Europe opposed France, for one reason or another, and France was always outnumbered.

Napoleon came to power with France still torn by its recent revolution. It was the liberating ideas of this revolution, spreading to adjacent nations, that brought to France wave after wave of royalist armies intent on stamping out this threat to the crowned heads of Europe. Napoleon had to consolidate his power in a democratically minded France while neutralizing the armies of his nervous neighbors.

THE SOLUTION

Napoleon was a unique individual in that he had numerous talents, and he knew how to use them without tripping over himself. This was a rare skill for someone of his enormous intellectual gifts. Ultimately, he failed, for he was unable to deal with an overabundance of ambition and confidence. The lesson here is, take your own press releases with a grain of salt.

Meanwhile, consider well the marvelous talents and techniques used successfully during his two decades of power.

★ The organizer. One of the major obstacles to mobilizing sufficient military power to support Napoleon's wars was the poorly organized government of France. So Napoleon had the government reformed, big time, with the introduction of the Napoleonic Code in 1804. This was a remarkable feat, one that had been in the works for a decade before Napoleon came along. France, along with all the world's other countries, had to deal with the problem of creating nations out of numerous ancient feudal entities, each with their existing laws and customs. Prerevolutionary France was no different, with different legal systems and commercial codes in each of its many regions. The French Revolution made Napoleon's task easier by sweeping away the aristocracy and their ancient feudal rights. But the commoners, especially the mercantile class, still clung to their local laws and practices. Facing a situation similar to what corporate executives must face after a merger, Napoleon moved quickly, decisively, and diplomatically to knit the different systems together. He also had the wisdom and patience to enlist, and effectively use, others who had long been working on a unified national legal code and were quite good at it. But Napoleon was the prime mover in actually getting the code completed successfully and put into practice. In 1807 the civil code was renamed the Code Napoléon, the name it has been known by ever since. The Code was Napoleon's most lasting achievement, and he himself was aware of its dramatic impact. The influence of the Code was worldwide, as it provided a dramatic example of how a universal legal code could be created for a nation with scores of different legal systems. The basic Code Napoléon is still used in France, and variations in many other countries.

★ The consolidator. Napoleon knew how to draw together resources to create powerful concentrations of administrative, political, or military power. He was known for this in his military campaigns, but he practiced the same technique in running the French government and mobilizing his foreign allies. Militarily, he developed techniques that allowed his troops, moving over a wide area, rapidly to concentrate at a point where the French army would do the most damage to the enemy. Administratively, Napoleon organized his government so he had trusted people running the parts and the ability to get all these administrators to work together to produce a new army, implement a new tax system, or carry out some other nationwide policy. With his foreign allies, he employed a carrot-and-stick approach more successfully than most practitioners. But the result was typically Napoleonic. For the invasion of Russia in 1812, Napoleon massed over six hundred thousand troops. Most of them were from his many allies in Europe, a truly multinational force. But because Napoleon managed to gather so many allied troops for this invasion, the disaster that followed was not as catastrophic for France as it might have been if most of the invading troops were French.

★ The perfectionist. Napoleon's first intellectual passion was mathematics, a discipline that sought perfection in its methods and results.

Napoleon applied his skills for calculating and finding the most efficient solution to everything he did. Sort of like a scientist becoming the head of a large corporation. Napoleon diligently reorganized the French government and, to a lesser extent, the national economy, by carefully planning and implementing each move. He left nothing, as far as he could, to chance. This approach was remarkably effective, especially since these systematic methods had not yet come into general use. The age of scientific management had not quite arrived yet and Napoleon benefited from being ahead of the pack. Napoleon's methodical approach to his military campaigns is more widely acknowledged. Where his enemies muddled through their military operations, improvising as they went, Napoleon developed a plan and methodically executed it. This enabled him to call the shots, or "take the initiative," as the military tended to describe it. Napoleon usually operated ahead of the curve when it came to management ideas and techniques. He made these methods work, even if no one had ever heard of them before.

★ Knowing your allies and dealing with them effectively. Napoleon was a shrewd judge of people, from common soldiers to kings and emperors. Dealing with the troops in his army was easy compared to the diplomacy he conducted with his many aristocratic enemies. But Napoleon was up to the challenge and for nearly twenty years he was able to convince, cajole, and bully the crowned heads of Europe into doing things Bonaparte's way. Napoleon did not do this solely with his considerable personal charm. He studied his opponents carefully and used an extensive network of spies, informants, and diplomats to collect information. A staff of experts in Paris organized this information and ensured that Napoleon, unlike many of his opponents, never went into negotiations unprepared. The downside of this was that Napoleon came to overestimate the power of his diplomatic tools. By the time he had overreached himself, it was too late to recover. Napoleon's diplomatic techniques were a good example of what happens when one doesn't keep things in perspective. What worked well once won't work the same way forever.

★   ★   ★

★ Maximizing the use of available resources. Although Napoleon's principal enemies had over three times France's population, and over twice France's GDP, Napoleon managed to match and defeat most of their military assaults on him. Napoleon did this by making the most of his resources. He raised two million troops during his time in power, and most of these were volunteers, as well as being better-quality manpower than what his opponents were using. This was about 6 percent of the available population. Twentieth-century nations have built armies with over twice that percentage of their population, but Napoleon was the first one to pull off a modern mass mobilization. Note that the American Civil War saw some three million troops raised from roughly the same population Napoleon had to work with. The intervening forty-five years had seen an enormous amount of industrialization in America and Europe, which accounted for the larger mobilization in the Civil War. But at the time, Napoleon's effort was the most awesome Europe had ever seen.

★ Propaganda. Napoleon was one of the first modern rulers to appreciate how powerful mass media could be. Mass media were only getting started during Napoleon's time. True mass media did not arrive for another twenty years, in the form of steam-driven printing presses that could cheaply turn out millions of newspapers, pamphlets, posters, and books. But Napoleon saw what was coming and knew the limited-edition newspapers available were widely read by the most politically active people. So he regularly issued bulletins while on campaign and controlled the press to the extent that these bulletins were given favorable display and comment in the newspapers. While not at war, he ensured that press releases from the government were written in plain language. He sometimes wrote these official announcements himself. Napoleon was always careful with his public image and public opinion in general. Although he declared himself an emperor, he acted like a democrat when it came to what the public thought of him.

★ Political control. Napoleon made himself first consul, then consul for life and finally emperor because the chaotic political situation in postrevolution France made it difficult, and often impossible, to get decisions made or programs implemented. There were simply too many individualistic politicians involved. Getting himself elected dictator was only part of his plan for obtaining political control. For a dictator with too many political enemies had little power to get things done, and Napoleon had a large list of things he wanted to accomplish. So, to assure his political power, he bought off, charmed, or cowed most political leaders, or potential political leaders, in France. One reason for reestablishing the monarchy, with himself as emperor, was to enable him to use freely the old feudal trick of purchasing loyalty with grants of real estate and political power. Even France was not wealthy enough to make all these payoffs. Lands and titles from other kingdoms the French controlled were gathered for Napoleon's political cronies. All this largess worked, up to a point. When Napoleon was on a roll, his well-compensated generals and officials were indeed quite loyal. But when things got rough, they confronted him and forced him out in 1814. Loyalty was one thing, but losing all that real estate was something else. Yet most of the time Napoleon's techniques for political control worked quite well.

★ Decisiveness, big-league decisiveness. Napoleon rarely was at a loss for what to do and, when at a loss, was just as likely to jump right in and do something. This was quite a difference from most of his battlefield, and diplomatic, opponents. Napoleon was fortunate in that he went to war at a time when there was a severe shortage of decent military commanders in the rest of Europe. Against one of the hotshots of a generation or two earlier, like Frederick the Great of Prussia or Suvarov of Russia, some of Napoleon's decisiveness might have been reinterpreted as rashness. But there was sufficient method and planning in Napoleon's decisiveness to protect him from an equally energetic opponent. What eventually brought Napoleon down was subordinates who were unable to keep up with the boss. While Napoleon's opponents got better as the years went by, no one ever came close to Napoleon in terms of decision-making prowess. But for the most part, Napoleon used his decisiveness wisely and effectively.

★ ★ ★

★ Enthusiasm for combat. Napoleon was a child of the military, having received all his education in military schools. He went straight from the military schools to the French army as a teenage officer. Napoleon loved it. Napoleon bought into the idea that a lot of complicated social problems could be solved with a few decisive battles. He managed to get off to a good start in his combat career. Mainly, he didn't get killed doing the risky things junior officers are expected to do to get recognized. Napoleon was a brilliant thinker who came along just when several generations of military innovators had come up with some really useful ideas. For example, the modern method of organizing combat units (brigades, divisions, corps, etc.) and the dominance of artillery were just coming into fashion when Napoleon came on the scene. These two concepts made Napoleon's form of warfare possible. Napoleon's enthusiasm for military operations, coupled with his talent for it and effective techniques, made Napoleon's numerous military operations rather inevitable.

★ Compromise (If you can't beat 'em, join 'em.) Napoleon was a member of the aristocracy. Granted, his ancestors were nobles in Corsica and Italy, for the most part, but aristocrats nonetheless. Napoleon, like many other nobles who comprised the majority of the officers in the royal army, remained with his unit when the royal army turned into the republican army in the early 1790s. Being a twenty-year-old lieutenant and a member of the minor Corsican nobility, Napoleon was not seen as a potential royalist traitor to the republican revolution. Napoleon did believe many of the revolutionary ideas when he was young, and was able to convince royalists and republicans that he was foursquare for the revolution. But once Napoleon became the head of the French government in 1799, and arranged to give himself dictatorial powers, he began to see the advantages of a kingship. So he convinced most people in France it would be a good idea to return to monarchy. Napoleon crowned himself (with the pope in attendance) emperor in 1804. All of this was not just for French consumption; Napoleon hoped to convince the other kings and emperors in Europe that France and its new emperor were no longer a threat to

European royalists and the feudal governments over which they presided. In 1810 he married the daughter of the Austrian emperor. While Napoleon did manage to garner some goodwill among the European aristocrats, he could not paper over French domination of Europe and the lingering (and quite pervasive) republicanism among the French people and their government. The rest of Europe was willing to make a deal if Napoleon would stop grabbing territory adjacent to France and interfering in the politics of other nations. Napoleon could never bring himself just to run France, so his neighbors were never willing to stop fighting him.

★ Charm. While basically a shy person, Napoleon realized the personal touch could overcome a lot of problems. His personality was pleasant, and he developed a rather effective personal charm as he became older and more powerful. Even his enemies were impressed by Napoleon's capability to enchant them on a one-on-one basis. Napoleon used this skill often and with increasing effectiveness as he got older. He managed to combine his enormous power with this charisma into a powerful tool he used on individuals and groups. Many military leaders and civilian managers have used similar skills to great effect and will continue to.

★ The police state. Napoleon's France was the first modern police state. There were records kept on thousands of people considered potentially dangerous. Regular and secret police kept a tight lid on things. The media were closely controlled, as was the legal system. Napoleon's attitude was that he needed an orderly France in order to carry out his program and as long as he was successful and popular, his police state would not cause him any problems. As with most dictators, and control freaks in general, Napoleon was right in the short run. But long-term, the resentments built up. When he was down on his luck, he discovered a lot of people he had stepped on earlier were now out for revenge. Napoleon's reputation improved in the decades after his death, but immediately after his fall from power, many in France did not feel very charitable toward Napoleon and his government. The implications of this for managers is that the tools now available for monitoring employees have to be used carefully. The employee backlash against intrusive monitoring can be expensive in the long run, even though there are benefits from this control in the short run.

★ The antidemocratic democrat. Despite his authoritarian methods, Napoleon still operated like a democrat. That is, he paid close attention to public opinion and devoted a lot of effort to convincing people he had the common touch and cared about them personally. Not all dictators use this approach, but the more successful ones do. Managers usually have what could best be described as dictatorial powers, but in any organization, such power is best exercised with a light touch. It is prudent to act like a democrat, even though one is presiding over the equivalent of a police state.

Napoleon left a rich legacy for managers. At heart, Napoleon was a manager. While his battlefield exploits get most of the attention, his administrative accomplishments have had the most lasting effect on mankind. Napoleon was also one of the first modern technocrat managers. He trained in many scientific disciplines and was particularly fond of mathematics. He surrounded himself with scientists and engineers, and his outlook resembled that of a scientist. It is when he strayed from his careful calculations, as with his ill-planned invasion of Russia, that he got into trouble. But Napoleon was no stereotypical dork, geek, or propellor head. While shy by nature, he taught himself to overcome this and connect with people very successfully. When one studies Napoleon for management wisdom, all one has to do is look behind whatever Napoleon did, to see the marvelous details and methods developed by Bonaparte to accomplish the seemingly impossible.

CHAPTER 10

★ U. S. GRANT ★

THE TYCOON OF TURNAROUND

AMERICAN CIVIL WAR general Ulysses S. Grant was not as spectacular a field commander as many of his adversaries, particularly Robert E. Lee. But Grant was adept at rapidly turning around disastrous situations. Grant was the turtle that eventually won the race to victory against rabbits like Lee. Grant never succeeded at nonmilitary business, but in the chaos of war, he left a legacy of lessons that can still be learned from.

THE WORLD OF U. S. GRANT (1822–1885)

Ulysses Simpson Grant's birth on April 27, 1822, brought him into the world shortly after the War of 1812, and the end of Napoleon's rampage across Europe. The armies Grant would lead and the battles he fought would little resemble any of the great armies of conflicts of the past. Only the Napoleonic wars had been close in the size and scope of the Civil War, and yet they were much different in its substance. The Civil War had more in common with World War I than it did with the other wars of the nineteenth century. Grant, one might say, was the first twentieth-century general.

Grant was born to an Ohio businessman. Jesse Grant, Ulysses's father, was a tanner. Young Grant hated the sight and smell of the blood always present in and around the tannery, and he looked for opportunities to take himself away from his father's business. An opportunity came knocking in 1838, when his father came home and declared that

Ulysses was going to West Point. Grant at first hesitated, but warmed to it as he realized his father was committed to the idea, plus it would get him away from the tannery.

West Point was not like the older military institutions in Europe. It was very American. For one thing, cadets were appointed to the school in one of two ways. First, they could receive a political appointment, the way Ulysses was appointed. Second, some were admitted on ability alone. This differed from the European model where, for the most part, only the nobility and upper class were allowed to serve as officers. The Point also differed from its European counterparts in that the emphasis was on engineering and mathematics, rather than military history and pomp. West Point still had plenty of history and ceremony, but the best graduates traditionally went into the Corps of Engineers.

When Grant arrived at West Point the summer of 1839, his name (Hiram Ulysses Grant) underwent a change because of a clerical error. The congressman submitting his papers had forgotten Grant's first name. Grant himself disliked the name Hiram and had been referring to himself as Ulysses H. Grant. The congressman had filled the papers out as Ulysses Simpson Grant, remembering that his mother's maiden name was Simpson. Rather than fight it, Grant allowed the name change to stand and thus he became U. S. Grant. His friends at West Point tended to call him Sam Grant.

The name change, and setting the school equestrian jumping record at six feet three inches, were the most significant accomplishments of Grant's tenure at West Point. He did not distinguish himself academically. He graduated near the middle of his class. However, his time at West Point proved valuable to him in his Civil War years, as many of the generals he would fight with or against were fellow students.

After graduating from West Point in 1843, he was assigned to an infantry regiment. About the same time, he married Julia Dent, a sister of one his classmates. Julia was the anchor in Grant's life, and when he was away from her he missed her terribly. His separation from her would often drive him to drink.

Grant served uneventfully until the Mexican-American War of 1846. This conflict arose over decades of disagreements between the U.S. and Mexico. The principal dispute was over Texas, which was a part of Mexico until rebellions in the 1830s made it an independent nation. The nation of Texas later joined the U.S. as a state, and this eventually led to a war between the U.S. and Mexico. General Zachary Taylor led an army to the Rio Grande, the river separating Texas from Mexico. The officers accompanying Taylor, or joining him later, read like a Who's Who of Civil War leaders. General Winfield Scott, who later commanded all Union forces at the start of the Civil War, led another army that landed on the Mexican coast and marched on Mexico City.

After several small but successful battles, the United States annexed much of today's Southwest. Grant served in combat and noncombat jobs during the conflict and was twice promoted. He performed his duties well and distinguished himself several times. After the war he was posted to a garrison in California. To soothe the longing he felt for his wife, Julia, he took to the bottle. It is here he gained his reputation (rather exaggerated) for being a drunkard. Eventually the boredom and separation from Julia were too much. Grant resigned his commission in 1854 and returned to St. Louis, Missouri, where his wife and her family were living.

Grant slipped into obscurity, wandering from one job to the next. He tried farming, retailing, and government work, but success eluded him. At the start of the Civil War, local politicians became aware of his former army service. He was asked to help form a company of volunteers from the Galena, Illinois area (where Grant was living), but refused to serve as their captain, feeling it not proper for a former regular army captain to serve as a leader of militia volunteers. Finally, the shortage of experienced officers brought him command of an Illinois regiment, with the rank of colonel, in the spring of 1861. He did so well with his regiment that, in a few months, he was promoted to general and given command of a brigade. Grant was a natural soldier, and now he had a war to showcase his martial talents. His Civil War career had begun.

Grant's legacy is well known. His first fight would come at Belmont in the fall of 1861 with a force of a little over three thousand men. His last fight would come in the spring of 1865 at Appomattox. At the end of the Civil War he commanded over a million men. In between Belmont and Appomattox would be Forts Henry and Donelson, Shiloh, Iuka, Corinth, the Vicksburg Campaign, Chattanooga, and finally overall commander of the Union armies for the last year of the war. Grant's frequent promotions were simply recognition that he had a tendency to win nearly all his battles.

THE CHALLENGE

Grant would face a number of challenges along his way to Appomattox and ultimate victory in the Civil War. One major change in warfare during the mid nineteenth century was who led the armies. Prior to the nineteenth century, leaders like Alexander, Frederick the Great, Edward III, and others had both run their countries and led their troops into battle. Ever so slowly, the role of chief general and chief statesman had begun to separate. The generals of the nineteenth century, with exception of Napoleon and a few others, would execute state policy, not make it. Those that could not execute the policies of the politicians would be swept aside, replaced by others who could achieve the goals of the state.

During the course of the Civil War, a parade of commanding generals made their way through President Lincoln's office. Many of these men were very knowledgeable about military matters. What they lacked was the ability to fight and an understanding of how to get their military strategy in line with the political strategy of the president. Lincoln again and again had to replace his senior generals. None of these commanders seemed to know how to fight, much less win, a battle. As competent as Lincoln was as president, he could not govern the nation and run the military at the same time; he needed someone in uniform who could lead the Union armies to victory.

Another challenge was the makeup of the Union army. It was not a professional army. Rather, recent volunteers and conscripts filled the ranks. At the beginning of the Civil War, the regular army had only 15,000 troops. In addition to the regular army, there were the state militias. In the north there were 75,000 organized militia troops, and 40,000 in the Confederate States. By the end of the war over one million men would be in arms on the Union side alone, with another million having already served (360,000 of these died in service, the rest left for various reasons). Since most of the troops were raised by local state militia units, the first year or two of the war saw troops being trained largely by officers and NCOs with no military experience. Everyone learned the hard way that inexperienced troops were prone to making many mistakes in combat, mistakes that caused many more casualties.

Most officers were no more professional than the common soldier. The officer training school at West Point had, from its founding in 1802 to 1860, graduated 1,875 officers. These were the only professionally trained army officers in the country. There were several thousand other officers produced by on-the-job training. But by 1860, many of the West Pointers were already dead or too old for service. Only 746 would serve the Union and 396 the South. These numbers were nowhere near the quantity needed. Just before the war began, the 15,000-man U.S. Army had only 1,080 officers on active duty. By the time the war ended, nearly 200,000 officers would be commissioned on the Union side alone. Although West Point graduates rose quickly in rank, it turned out only about a third of the thousand generals on both sides were graduates of West Point. Even the pros were not all up to the challenge of a real war. Most of the Civil War officers were civilians, usually educated men or fellows prominent in their own communities, who raised units from among their neighbors and learned how to be army officers on the battlefield. Many died learning, as did many of their troops.

Adding to the problem of few trained officers, was the way both former officers and new officers were appointed to their commands. Since the Union relied on the states for volunteers, the appointment of the high brass was heavily influenced by the governors of the various states. Leaders not only had to succeed on the battlefield; they had to be politically correct for their day. This led to many officers taking command solely because of their political connections and not because of their military capabilities. Those with talent would have to be patient and wait for someone on the ball to notice them.

Another fundamental problem was that successful wartime leaders had personality characteristics making them less suitable for peacetime service. A good wartime officer is generally impatient and ruthless, and frequently a nonconformist as well. A good peacetime military leader is more of a manager and diplomat, and most definitely a team player.

In peacetime the people who don't quite fit in are likely to have very pedestrian careers. Many of the best Civil War leaders had been in the army, but had left the service looking for better opportunities in civilian life. For example, of the seven most successful American Civil War generals (Lee, Longstreet, Jackson, Grant, Sherman, Thomas, and Sheridan), three (Grant, Sherman, and Jackson) were civilians when the war broke out.

The last challenge Grant faced was technology and how it affected the Civil War battlefield. This was the first war ever fought in which sail power or muscle power did not dominate the waterways. Ships powered by steam could now move with ease and in any direction. Armor plating on ships became common during the Civil War. The numerous armored, steam-powered Union warships made rivers far more important than they had been in any previous war, and Grant took full advantage of this. It would be the first conflict fought in which railroads would be a dominant, and far superior, means of moving supplies. Grant was quick to use the railroads far more successfully than any other Civil War commander.

Arms and ammunitions had evolved to new levels. For several centuries, muskets had an effective range of a hundred yards. Now, with rifling and bullets of a new design, effective range was four to six hundred yards. In addition, the rate of fire was nearly doubled. Artillery also saw significant improvements. The telegraph was now available to improve greatly long-distance communications. This only scratches the surface of the technologies developed during the war. The Civil War was the first of the modern wars. No commander could be expected to understand and exploit all of these new technologies. But a good commander would at least see the advantages of some of them. Grant met the challenge of all this new technology, and therein lies his lessons for modern managers.

THE SOLUTION

To determine why Ulysses S. Grant was a successful commander is a daunting task. Of all of the military leaders we have studied so far, he is the most enigmatic. At first sight, Grant is plain and boring. He was an ordinary-looking man who did not play or dress the part of a general. He wore ordinary clothes and expected no special treatment. Many underestimated his capabilities because of the first impression he gave. But there lay a depth behind the plainness that makes Grant a great leader.

Grant mustered a potent arsenal of winning techinques.

★ Clear communication. An important trait of Grant's was his clear written communication. This skill was of tremendous importance in the Civil War. The size and the scope of the Civil War was unlike anything before it. Alexander, Edward III, Frederick the Great and the others we have studied were able to give most of their strategic orders face-to-face. Only rarely did their orders have to be carried over long distances. As the battles grew in size at the end of the eighteenth century and at the beginning of the nineteenth century, commanders were forced to write their orders down and have them carried to their subordinates. During the Civil War, these subordinates could be several hours, if not several days away (as the army marched, at about twenty miles a day). A commander had more complicated problems of time and space to consider when issuing these written orders, and had to understand his subordinates' quirks. For example, some subordinates would follow their orders rigidly, with no deviation. Others would be opportunistic, he could depend on them to make immediate use of unexpected opportunities they ran into. Many, if not most, Civil War generals had problems issuing clear, concise, and effective written orders. After the Civil War, the preparation of these battle orders would become an area of intense study for professional soldiers. But during the Civil War, a commander either had a natural talent for it, or he learned the hard way what worked and what didn't.

Grant handled most of his communications with his subordinates himself. In his communications he was always clear. He would tell his subordinates about the details he felt were most important, then leave the rest to them. He was always certain about the final objective of the order.

Many Civil War generals made the mistake of writing open-ended orders. Or they would assume too much. Grant's orders were always precise and to the point. Grant did not obscure the facts with flowery words or phrases. The following are orders given to Sherman on the May 16, 1863, prior to the Battle of Champion's Hill, one of the battles fought during the Vicksburg Campaign:

> *Start one of your divisions on the road at once with its ammunition wagons—and direct it to move with all possible speed till it comes up with our rear beyond Bolton. It is important that great celerity should be shown in carrying out this movement, as I have evidence that the entire force of the enemy was at Edward's Depot 7 o'clock yesterday evening and still advancing. The fight might be brought on at any moment—we should have every man on the field.*

General Mead said this about Grant's orders, "There is one striking feature . . . no matter how hurriedly he may write them on the field, no one ever has the slightest doubt as to their meaning, or ever has to read them over a second time to understand them."

★ Optimist. Grant was a great optimist. This optimism carried him throughout the war. Time after time Grant would appear to be defeated, but his optimism never let him quit. An example of Grant's optimism showed itself at the Battle of Shiloh (early April, 1862). Grant and his troops were buoyed by the victories of Fort Henry and Fort Donelson during February. The main body of his troops had moved to an area just west of the Tennessee River and north of a small church named Shiloh. Grant chose this place to move his troops to because of the good road network leading to Corinth, Mississippi, where the Confederate troops were concentrated. Grant forgot the Confederates could use the road system just as well. Therefore, when the Confederates attacked on the morning of April 6, the Union forces were not prepared. By the end of the day the Union camps had been overrun, and the troops had been pushed to the breaking point.

Two incidents that evening showed Grant's optimism and confidence in action. First, Lieutenant Colonel J. B. McPherson asked Grant if he intended to retreat. Grant, annoyed with the question, replied, "No, I purpose to attack at daylight and whip them." Later in the evening General Sherman found Grant standing under a tree smoking a cigar. Sherman went to ask him to reconsider the retreat proposed earlier by McPherson. But on seeing Grant, he thought better of it. Instead Sherman said, "Well, Grant, we've had the devil's own day, haven't we."

"Yes," said Grant. "Yes. Lick 'em tomorrow, though." And Grant did.

It was this optimistic attitude that set Grant apart from his contemporaries. Where other generals saw defeat, Grant saw victory. Where other generals saw problems, Grant saw solutions. This was the mark of a natural leader.

★ Solution oriented. Abraham Lincoln described Grant's attitude for finding solutions instead of problems in the following manner:

I am glad to find a man that can go ahead without me. When any of the rest set out on a campaign, they would look over matters and pick out some one thing they were short of and they knew I couldn't give 'em and tell me they couldn't hope to win unless they had it; and it was most generally cavalry. Now, when Grant took hold, I was waiting to see what his pet impossibility would be, and I reckoned it would be cavalry, of course, for we hadn't horses enough to mount what men we had. There were fifteen thousand or there abouts up near Harper's Ferry and no horses to put them on. Well, the other day, Grant sends to me about those very men, just as I expected; but what he wanted to know was whether he could make infantry of them or disband 'em. He doesn't ask impossibilities of me, and he's the first general I have had that didn't.

An example of how Grant approached problems occurred during the Battle of the Wilderness in 1864. Once again the battle had become desperate for the Union troops. At this time Grant was now facing the famous Robert E. Lee. Lee had reached cult status at this time on both sides of the fighting. One of Grant's generals, in a panic, said to Grant, "General Grant, this is a crisis that cannot be looked upon too seriously. I know Lee's methods well by past experience; he will throw his whole army between us and the Rapidan, and cut us off completely from communications."

Grant took his ever-present cigar from his mouth and proceeded to educate the officer on the attitude he himself had and that he desired in his subordinates: "Oh, I am heartily tired of hearing about what Lee is going to do. Some of you always seem to think he is suddenly going to turn a double somersault and land in our rear and on both of our flanks at the same time. Go back to your command and try to think what we are going to do ourselves, instead of what Lee is going to do."

★ Innovation. By his own admission Grant was not a great scholar of military affairs. This, however, was one of his strengths. Grant did not attempt to fight his battles based on lessons and principles from previous wars. He wrote in his memoirs that "war is progressive." Grant had grasped the fact that warfare changed as technology and society changed. This allowed him to innovate and not to try to fight his battles like Napoleon or other great generals had. Many Civil War generals were still operating in the past. They were always thinking about how Napoleon would have done it. Grant did it the way Grant would have done it.

One of his first innovations was the use of naval transportation and support. At one of his first battles, Belmont, Grant used the navy steamboats to move his troops quickly, rather than marching overland. In addition Grant had the steam-driven gunboats *Tyler* and the *Lexington* maneuver and fire on the Confederate batteries to distract them. Even though the battle as a whole was a failure, the use of naval assets was a success. Before steam-powered ships, Grant's maneuvers would have been impossible.

Grant would next use the navy at Fort Henry February 6, 1862. Because of the navy's success at Belmont, Grant felt Fort Henry could be defeated by naval gunfire alone and that the army could be used to cut off the fleeing troops. This was a unique view for an army officer. It almost worked. If Grant's troops had not struggled getting into place, they would have been able to prevent the retreat of the Confederates from Fort Henry. Grant continued to use naval forces throughout his campaigns whenever possible.

Another innovation of Grant's was a raid-oriented strategy. This was a concept that he had developed in concert with William Tecumseh Sherman. Throughout the war, Grant and Sherman debated how to defeat the South, and finally realized that in order to bring the South to its knees, they would have to attack the heart of the South. Grant and Sherman saw that by attacking the South's logistical centers, their transportation networks, and the people, they could crush the South's war-making capability. This was a major jump away from the way wars had traditionally been fought. Armies battled other armies. The goal was to seek out and destroy the commander on the field. Grant and Sherman determined to destroy the South in their homes, to destroy their means, and will, to fight.

Sherman's March through Georgia, starting in November 1864, was the culmination of this raid-oriented theory. When Sherman began his march through the South, it was to carry out Grant's plan. To cut oneself off from supply lines, like Sherman did, was a violation of every principle of warfare at the time. But, as Grant and Sherman had learned at Vicksburg, the South was so rich in foodstuffs that an army could forage and survive off the land. Grant and Sherman's willingness to innovate and to think out of the box probably prevented the Civil War from dragging on for another year or two, and resulted in the unconditional surrender of the South.

★ Daring. Shortly after the Civil War began, Richard Ewell, soon to become one of the South's leading generals and to lose one of his legs for the Cause, was discussing the North's potential leadership. He remarked:

> There is one West Pointer, I think in Missouri, little known, and whom I hope the Northern people will not find out. I mean Sam Grant. I knew him well at the academy and in Mexico. I should fear him more than any of their officers I have yet heard of. He is not a man of genius, but he is clearheaded, quick and daring.

Ewell described the one quality that more than any other set Grant apart from his contemporary generals, daring. Most of the top-level brass of the war would prepare and prepare their troops for battle, but were deathly afraid of doing anything that would lose them a battle. This drove Lincoln to many sleepless nights.

Grant was not of the same cloth. If he saw the opportunity to win, he seized it. Grant would take risks.

Grant exhibited a large amount of daring during the Vicksburg Campaign. The town of Vicksburg, Mississippi, sat on a bend of the Mississippi River. This allowed anyone holding the place to control the flow of river traffic. Union forces had won a series of victories that put them in a position that, if they could capture Vicksburg, would allow them to control the entire river and cut the Confederacy off from Texas.

The area surrounding Vicksburg was a quagmire of rivers and marshes. The best approaches were from either the east or the south of the town. Troops could not be moved down the river via transport, as they would be easy targets of the Vicksburg artillery. Grant could pull his troops back toward Memphis, Tennessee, and try a different approach to Vicksburg. That would have resulted in political fallout that would have demoralized the North and caused problems. Grant spent several months trying to attack from the current position of his forces in Vicksburg, the west side of the river and north of the town. This included trying to cut a canal through the bend in order to transport troops down the river below Vicksburg. None of these attempts succeeded. Finally, Grant decided to move his troops down the west side of the river, and then move naval forces and empty transports rapidly past Vicksburg's guns. Once both naval and army forces were below Vicksburg, the land forces would board the transports, cross the Mississippi, and march northeast, to attack Vicksburg from the west.

This plan meant that the Union forces would be cut off from their lines of supplies and communications. This was a daring and dangerous course of action; if Grant's plan failed, it would mean the loss of all his forces. Grant could see no other alternatives at the time and decided to roll the dice. Ulysses's daring proved too much for Confederate forces, and Vicksburg surrendered.

★ Calm during chaos. Perhaps the true genius of Grant was his ability to function normally under conditions of great stress and confusion. When there was confusion all around, Grant continued to operate as if there was none.

An example of Grant's calmness amid confusion happened during the Wilderness Campaign shortly after he took command of all the Union forces in the spring of 1864. Grant had gone out to supervise the battle that was raging. After taking in the situation, Grant sat down on a tree stump to write a dispatch to one of his generals. While he was writing the dispatch, an artillery shell exploded overhead. Grant looked up from his writing. After a pause he continued the dispatch. One soldier who witnessed this event remarked to his commanding officer: "Ulysses don't scare worth a damn."

When most generals would have panicked, Grant remained calm. This attribute let him remain in control of the situation instead of the situation controlling him.

★ Focus and persistence. Once Grant had a goal in mind he was not distracted from it. He would continue toward the goal and not turn back. Stories are told of his traveling toward a destination on horseback. If he found that road was not taking him where he wanted to go, he would begin jumping fences and streams looking for a new route. He would not turn back, and he would not give up.

The Vicksburg Campaign described above is an example of his focus and persistence. He exhibited this trait when he took over the armies in the east. Time and time again the Army of the Potomac, the major army group in the east during the Civil War, attacked Lee. Many of these attacks never resulted in much more than draws. Grant did not give up and did not step back. His goal was the destruction of Lee's army. After a battle, Grant would adjust his plans and attack again. Finally, he was victorious at Appomattox, forcing Lee into an unconditional surrender.

★ Trusted assistants. During the war Grant's staff was made up of men he could trust to get the job done. Many of them were from Illinois. One of these men, John A. Rawlins, a lawyer in his hometown, became Grant's protector and conscience. Many thought Rawlins was insubordinate at times, as he would take the general to task for various problems, like his drinking. Rawlins always had Grant's best interests at heart and protected the general from a multitude of political dangers. Rawlins also took much of the administrative load off the general.

Another trusted subordinate was William T. Sherman. Sherman would say of Grant and his relationship, "He stood by me when I was crazy, and I stood by him when he was drunk; and now, sir, we stand by each other always." Sherman had had a temporary mental breakdown. After Sherman had been restored to command, Grant gave him the chances, and trust, he needed to succeed.

Sherman was the antithesis of Grant. Where Grant was quiet and still, Sherman was gregarious and full of energy. Where Grant was a man of horse sense, Sherman was an intellectual. Where Grant hid his emotions, Sherman wore his on his sleeve. But the two men developed a trust in each other. At times Sherman vehemently opposed Grant's plans. An example of this opposition happened at Vicksburg; Sherman thought it was insane to cut one's own supply lines, but eventually he would do the same in his Atlanta campaign. Sherman, though, always supported Grant once the decision was made. Because Grant trusted Sherman, Sherman was often allowed to operate independently with great success. The two opposites formed a devastating team.

★ Modesty with strength. Grant has to be one of the most modest men ever to wear four stars on his shoulders. He never expected special treatment. This type of attitude endeared him to his troops and his subordinates. It also made it easier for him to get along with superiors. The modesty, at times, was seen as a lack of ambition. This was not the case. Grant was ambitious, but he did not let his ambition show.

Grant's modesty did not mean that he rolled over and let others' opinions carry the day. Grant listened to all ideas and comments. At the end of the day, the decisions were his. This modesty with strength was a powerful combination that caused great devotion to Grant. The lack of pretentiousness in Grant's character made it easier for the common man to follow Grant into battle.

The above traits only scratch the surface of the plain-looking man from Galena, Illinois. The longer you look at Grant, the more depth you find. If Grant, in his civilian life, had had a Rawlins or a Sherman as his partner to save him from himself, or if Grant had found a goal he could have committed himself to as much as he committed himself to the destruction of the South, he could have been as successful as a businessman and a politician as he had been as a general. Grant was one of those leaders who only attained peak performance when faced with the most dire challenges. Namely, war. Historically, this was not unusual. For many great military commanders have found themselves adrift and incapable of exceptional achievement during peacetime. In the past, such leaders were usually kings and thus able to keep the wars going. But from the nineteenth century on, this was less likely. With command of the nation and command of the armies now jobs held by different people, the generals either had to suffer the boredom of peacetime soldiering or stumble about in a civilian career. Such was the fate of U. S. Grant, who even as president of the United States was unable to recapture the challenges, and motivation, of the battle-field.

CHAPTER II

★ DOUGLAS MACARTHUR ★
COPING WITH DISASTER

MACARTHUR ACCOMPLISHED MUCH in the first half of the twentieth century, performing heroically in two World Wars, between those wars, and into the 1950s. Yet his most spectacular successes came right on the heels of his most crushing defeats. He knew how to deal with disaster. But MacArthur also knew how to deal with the media; indeed, he was ahead of his time in this respect. MacArthur had a rich bag of management tricks, most of which can still be profitably recycled. MacArthur was also a high-profile leader, and this led to his reputation in the popular mind being decidedly mixed. While MacArthur knew how to use the media, he also did not shy from taking on the press. This made him a lot of enemies, who responded by using their media access to leave a mixed record of what MacArthur was, what he did, and how he did. MacArthur never heeded the old adage, "Never argue with anyone who buys ink by the barrel."

THE WORLD OF DOUGLAS MACARTHUR (1880–1964)

Douglas MacArthur was the son of an American Civil War general (Arthur) and the grandson of a Scots immigrant who became a prominent lawyer and pillar of the Democratic party. Arthur MacArthur was born in 1845 and entered the Union army as a teenage lieutenant. In three years he earned the Medal of Honor and the command of a regiment. Arthur MacArthur left the army after the war ended, but found that he preferred the military life. In 1866 he rejoined, and over the next thirty years worked his way back up the ranks. By 1900, in the wake of the Spanish-American War, General Arthur MacArthur commanded U.S. forces in the Philippines. There was a savage war in the Philippines after the Americans replaced the Spanish. Some of the resistance was in favor of Philippines independence. Other factions fought to be separate from the Philippines. Arthur MacArthur presided over a bloody, but lasting, victory over all factions.

Arthur MacArthur's son, Douglas, was born on a United States Army base in 1880. Douglas was an army brat throughout his childhood. He greatly admired his father and wished to emulate his father's military record. Thus Douglas graduated from the United States Military Academy at West Point in 1903.

This was an exciting time to enter U.S. military service. While the Spanish-American war of 1898 was called, at the time, "a splendid little war," it also revealed a serious lack of professionalism in the American officer corps. As a result there was a burst of reform and rethinking in the U.S. Army between 1898 and World War I (1914). But there wasn't much opportunity for Lieutenant Douglas MacArthur to, like his father, see a lot of combat and get a Medal of Honor. Arthur MacArthur died in 1912, leaving his son Douglas disappointed that he did not have a chance to show his father what a great soldier his son could be. MacArthur apparently never forgot this desire to please his father, for over the succeeding decades he would frequently mention how much his father would have liked this or that of his son's military accomplishments. MacArthur always lived in his father's shadow. MacArthur's mother, who lived into the 1930s, also had a galvanizing effect on his ambitions, just as she had on her husband.

From 1903 to 1912, MacArthur had a variety of assignments, including an opportunity to spend some time in the Philippines with his father. MacArthur was noted as a very able young officer. But being young and talented, he also gave an impression of arrogance to some senior officers. This was something that MacArthur would continue to do throughout his career, even as he turned in outstanding performances on and off the battlefield.

In 1914, U.S. forces intervened in the Mexican Civil War. This gave MacArthur an opportunity to strut his stuff, and this he did in exceptional fashion. MacArthur's heroic exploits at Vera Cruz did not get him the desired Medal of Honor because the American commander, General Pershing, did not approve of the irregular methods MacArthur used (he led a daring raid that captured three locomotives from one Mexican faction) and was generally quite stingy giving out decorations. But these adventures did get noticed.

By the end of 1914, Lieutenant MacArthur was Captain MacArthur. And in 1916 he became Major MacArthur and was working in Washington as army liaison with the media. MacArthur showed a particular skill in dealing with journalists, and this experience was to prove invaluable throughout his career. MacArthur was one of the first military men deliberately to use the mass media and manipulate them to suit his own goals. MacArthur also knew how to place himself in the center of the action.

When America entered World War I in 1917, MacArthur managed to get involved in organizing one of the first divisions to go overseas (the 42nd, "Rainbow," division). MacArthur went to France as a colonel and the chief of staff of the division. In the course of World War I, he got promoted to brigadier general and commanded a brigade and ultimately the entire division. MacArthur believed in leading from out front. He was wounded several times and ended the war the most decorated officer in the United States Army.

In further recognition of MacArthur's talents, he was appointed superintendent of West Point in 1919, a plum assignment. But Pershing was now the chief of staff of the army and not too fond of MacArthur. So in 1922 MacArthur was assigned to a dead-end job in the Philippines. He managed to survive this, got promoted to major general in 1924, and was appointed chief of staff of the army in 1930. MacArthur knew how to play the political game as well as the battlefield one.

MacArthur came to run the army at a critical time. America was in the midst of the Great Depression (1929–1941) and he had to deal with a steadily shrinking budget. At the time, the United States Army was smaller than the Marine Corps is today. Moreover, the army was being called upon to help "battle" the Depression by providing officers and troops to run the Civilian Conservation Corps (a make-work program). These tasks were carried out with his customary efficiency. MacArthur even managed to get along with both the Republican president Hoover and the new Democratic president Roosevelt. But the job was not without cost. Ordered to evict unemployed World War I veterans camped out near the Capitol demanding a "bonus," MacArthur took the heat for following his orders. He also stirred up a lot of army officers and politicians by resisting calls for a separate air force, while still being an enthusiastic and knowledgeable advocate of air power.

In 1935, MacArthur became commander of the Philippine armed forces. The American government had decided to give the Philippines its independence in 1946. But from 1935 on there would be a period of self-rule under American supervision. Thus the desire by the Philippine leadership to hire a noted American military man to, quite literally, create the Philippine armed forces. MacArthur took the job for a number of reasons. Being chief of staff of the United States Army was as high as he could go in America. The Filipinos offered him a lot more money and the rank of field marshal. Moreover, the challenge of creating new armed forces from scratch was the sort of formidable undertaking that MacArthur relished. There was also the Japanese threat, for even in 1935 Japan was looming as the major aggressor in the Pacific. MacArthur was one of the U.S. military leaders who recognized the Japanese threat and were keen to do something about it. Defending the Philippines seemed to fit that bill.

MacArthur had spent much of his time as U.S. Army chief of staff trying to obtain funds to train his troops adequately. Unlike many peacetime generals who paid more attention to buying equipment than in developing troops' skills, MacArthur believed that the man, not weapon, was the decisive item on the battlefield. In the Philippines he found that he had even less money than when he was commanding American troops. Moreover, his Filipino troops spoke many different languages and few of them were experienced soldiers who could teach the others. To MacArthur, this simply made it more of a challenge. Besides, he had access to American air and naval power. He planned on overcoming any problems with organizing the Filipino forces by 1946. Meanwhile, the Japanese threat grew. Thus, in July 1941, MacArthur left Philippine service, returned to the U.S. military, and was appointed commander of U.S. forces in the Philippines and surrounding areas.

The Japanese attacked in December 1941. MacArthur's performance in the subsequent campaign was not one of his finer moments. Nevertheless, there wasn't much chance of MacArthur's winning the 1942 battle for the Philippines no matter how few mistakes he made. Until new U.S. warships came into service during 1943, Japan would control the waters around the Philippines. Not even the huge Japanese losses in the June 1942 Battle of Midway would change that. MacArthur resigned himself to capture or death in combat as he commanded the hard-fighting U.S. and Filipino troops holding out even though cut off from resupply and reinforcement. But America needed a hero, and Australia needed a tangible sign that the Allies would defend them. So President Roosevelt ordered MacArthur out of the Philippines in early March 1942, in order to assume command of all Allied forces in the area.

MacArthur's troops in the Philippines held out until May of 1942, the longest any of the Allied armies in the Pacific had resisted the Japanese that year. Meanwhile, the Japanese kept moving south, and Australia was in a panic. MacArthur made his stand in New Guinea, a large island just to the north of Australia. This battle hung in the balance for most of 1942. It wasn't until early 1943 that the Japanese were finally overcome. Meanwhile, an equally fierce battle was being fought to the east on Guadalcanal Island. This campaign had been undertaken by the U.S. Navy, even though Guadalcanal was in MacArthur's area of responsibility. MacArthur had to compete with U.S. Navy ambitions as well as the Japanese. He managed to deal with both effectively, although not without a lot of pyrotechnics.

This pointed up one of the major problems America had during World War II in the Pacific. The army and navy had a hard time agreeing on who was in charge. The navy had always seen the Pacific as its exclusive responsibility. The army had to be called in to put down the 1898–1901 Philippine rebellion, and remained to supply a small garrison. The army also had seen constant action against the Moslem rebels in the southern Philippines, a group that is still fighting to this day. But beyond another small army garrison in Hawaii, the navy represented America in the Pacific. After Pearl Harbor, the navy assumed it would run the show. It assumed wrong. Roosevelt needed someone with a reputation to command the troops defending Australia. There were no navy admirals who fit the bill, and only one army general—MacArthur. Former chief of staff, most decorated officer of World War I, and currently commanding the Philippine forces battling the Japanese, MacArthur was the obvious choice. Yet the navy saw to it that MacArthur only got a (relatively) small part of the Pacific, basically the area from Australia to the Philippines. The navy had all the rest. Which was a lot, as the Pacific covers a third of the planet's surface.

What followed was the portion of MacArthur's life that is most well-known to Americans. He ably led his troops north from Australia, retook the Philippines, and, in the last week of the war, was given command of all Allied forces in the Pacific. Most importantly, he was put in charge of Japan after the war and turned the devastated nation away from its militaristic ways. This was no small accomplishment and one of the things MacArthur was most proud of.

The last act in MacArthur's life saw him being called back, at age seventy, to command UN troops resisting a Communist North Korean invasion. This went brilliantly for a few months. But then MacArthur misjudged Chinese intentions, followed by his troops being chased south again. An ensuing argument with his commander in chief (President Truman) led to MacArthur being removed from command in April 1951. But he came home a hero, for he had not been home in sixteen years. He dabbled in politics, but basically lived quietly until his death, in 1964, as the century's most respected American military hero. His farewell address to a joint session of Congress closed with a line from a World War I British army song: "Old soldiers never die; they simply fade away."

There wasn't a dry eye in the house, which was exactly what Douglas MacArthur intended.

THE CHALLENGE

MacArthur had a life full of challenges, never flinching from taking on crises that scared away or defeated other commanders. But the challenge MacArthur paid the most attention to was one that few people were aware of. You have to keep in mind that MacArthur was essentially a nineteenth-century man. Although his fifty-two-year-long military career was largely in the twentieth century, he maintained decidedly nineteenth century ideas of how a military commander should operate. He felt honor and glory were the most worthy goals for a soldier. His first priority, and principal challenge, was maintaining his reputation as a soldier. This meant that he not only had to win battles, but had to win more spectacular victories than other commanders, friend or foe.

MacArthur was nothing but a soldier, and one of the old school at that. He served his master, the United States, and sought to bring honor and glory to himself and his country by being the most successful general of his century, if not several others. MacArthur set himself quite a challenge and went a long way toward meeting it.

THE SOLUTION

Among the many generals of the twentieth century, MacArthur was arguably the best endowed with those skills and talents a military commander needs most. He had quite a collection of abilities, the most notable of which are discussed below.

★ Putting on a show. From his earliest battlefield experience, in 1914, MacArthur dressed and acted in a distinctive manner. He wanted to be noticed in the chaos of the battlefield, and he was. As an officer in combat, this had advantages. For a fearless and competent officer like MacArthur, these mannerisms reassured the troops and made it easier for the soldiers to find their leader. The eccentric dress and props like the corncob pipe made MacArthur stand out. While these habits served MacArthur well in his early days, as he became a senior officer, he was often held up to ridicule by the media. What works on the battlefield doesn't always work on the front page of a newspaper. But MacArthur was consistent in his habits, and his showmanship resonated with many of the newspapers' readers, even if it offended the sensibilities of some journalists. The troops also appreciated MacArthur's distinctive getup when he visited them at the front. The lesson here is to know who your audience is and play to it. There's a lesson here for ambitious managers. If you want to stand out from your peers, do something to get noticed. If this can work in as regimented an organization as the U.S. Army, then it should be possible in any company.

★ Grasping the details. MacArthur was a staff officer for many years, and he had no problem dealing with the mass of details such work entailed. He was one of those people who absorbed detail and was able to trot it out later as needed. As warfare became increasingly more technical in the twentieth century, MacArthur's capacity for technical detail made him better able to stay on top of things. Many of his contemporaries were not able to maintain the pace, which is one reason why MacArthur was always the oldest general still in the harness.

★ Keeping up with technology. MacArthur was one of the biggest fans of technology among World War II generals. He was low-key about it, but with his subordinates he was always pushing for more use of current high tech and new weapons in general. He encouraged his commanders to take chances with new ideas. This led to a lot of innovations in the use of air power and amphibious operations by MacArthur's troops. This particular trait is even more needed today, as technology now advances even faster than it did during World War II. Much of MacArthur's success came from his astute use of new technology.

★ Making the media work for you. Early in his career, MacArthur had been assigned to deal with the media for the entire U.S. Army. He found this assignment much to his liking and picked up insights on how to deal with the press that served him well for the rest of his career. MacArthur's prowess with the press came from nothing more than knowing what kind of story the press was looking for and what angles the journalists were most likely to pursue, and taking advantage of the situation. He gave the media what they thought they wanted, and what MacArthur knew he wanted. MacArthur's relationship with the media was often a contentious one. Many journalists knew they were being manipulated, or thought they were even when they weren't, and went out of their way to slam MacArthur in their reporting. Other papers and broadcasters thought MacArthur was a swell guy. Your picture of MacArthur depended a lot on the newspaper you read or the radio commentator you listened to. Overall, though, MacArthur got across the point that he was a power to be reckoned with, and that was his main point. As many managers have discovered, gaining press notoriety can be a double-edged sword. The media are fickle, as MacArthur discovered. Yesterday's hero can become today's villain, with film at eleven.

★ Being charming. MacArthur was actually a rather shy fellow. But he was also quite personable in small groups and, if he had time to prepare, a masterful public speaker. MacArthur learned to use his considerable personal charm as needed. Most of the time, MacArthur came across as quite aloof. But when he had to, he could charm someone in a way the person would never forget. Whether it was an infantry private at the front line or President John Kennedy, when MacArthur turned on the charm, the person was truly and decidedly charmed. MacArthur used his charm to good effect when he had to, and he rarely failed to get what he wanted. His public speaking was also worthy of note. He had a splendid delivery and was, to use an ancient term, an accomplished orator. He could not speak all that well in front of an audience, off-the-cuff. But MacArthur did prepare excellent speeches when he had to, and then delivered them to excellent effect. Charm, with individuals and groups, was one of MacArthur's greatest assets. Modern managers can learn much from this. While fire-breathing executives often get most of the attention, it is the polite and charming ones who are more likely to get things done. The sweetness-and-light-type manager can still fire one's sorry ass for nonperformance. But the pleasant manager can also gain the confidence of subordinates more readily and have an easier time dealing with outsiders. Charm has its advantages, many of them.

★ Hiring the best. As bright and capable as MacArthur was, he realized that he could not do everything himself. So when he became senior enough to acquire high-ranking subordinates of his own, he went after the best. Through most of the 1930s, future president

Dwight Eisenhower was on MacArthur's staff. "Ike" was but one example of many. While many bright officers were repelled by MacArthur and his showbiz ways, many more were eager to work with someone who was clearly one of the more successful generals of the twentieth century. MacArthur was known throughout the army as a brilliant officer who expected much from his immediate subordinates. This attracted a lot of talent. MacArthur used talented people to the limits of their ability and provided exciting leadership. There were some negatives. MacArthur expected blind loyalty and would often play political games with his subordinates. For example, he tended not to tell subordinates what he thought their shortcomings were, but he reported those same faults to the Pentagon when it came time to decide who would get promoted. Despite his sometimes shabby treatment of his exceptional subordinates, he profited greatly by following the ancient practice of getting the best.

★ Tolerating human failings, up to a point. As talented and ambitious as MacArthur was, he was remarkably forgiving when it came to the shortcomings of the subordinates closest to him. These members of his staff and his most senior commanders, who saw MacArthur face-to-face on a regular basis, were treated a lot more leniently than those division and corps commanders who did not often see MacArthur in person. This latter group would be regularly treated with considerable callousness. MacArthur seemed to feel he knew his immediate subordinates well enough to justify making allowances for poor performance. With those he did not know as well, with the subordinates of his subordinates, he was much less patient or understanding. MacArthur provides modern managers with a useful lesson here. Managers can't always have the most capable people, and they have to either make allowances, or do something worse. Like trying to do the job themselves or doing without someone who is otherwise quite capable. MacArthur struck a useful balance in this area.

★ Being smarter than everyone else. MacArthur was born with considerable intelligence, and, with the constant urgings of his mother, he continued to develop himself intellectually. He never stopped reading or generally absorbing new information and sorting it out. In the smarts department, he did not rest on his laurels. Being smart is, by itself, not enough. People have to work at maintaining their mental edge. President John Kennedy visited the eighty-year-old MacArthur in 1961 and was pleasantly surprised at how charming and, more impressively, informed MacArthur was. As a former naval officer (MacArthur was always fighting the navy for resources) and a Democrat (the Republicans tended to adopt MacArthur as one of their own) Kennedy expected the worst. But, as he had done all his life, MacArthur defied the conventional wisdom on who he was and how he acted.

★ Demanding blind loyalty. MacArthur played a very political game, and could ill afford leaks and defections from his camp. Thus he was strict about personal loyalty. When a subordinate worked directly for MacArthur, he worked for no one else. The quickest way to get tossed off MacArthur's team was to get caught in a disloyal act (as defined by MacArthur, said definition could vary considerably depending on the individual and situation). The result was that MacArthur's crew was a loyal and trustworthy one. Whether from fear or conviction, MacArthur didn't care as long as his men were his and his alone. Here, MacArthur was following an ancient custom, one that is, today, more difficult to use. In the past commanders could hold an aide's family hostage to ensure loyalty. They can't do that today, although other sanctions are available. The most popular are stock options, vesting, and other forms of "golden chains."

★ The common touch. Part of the MacArthur charm was his ability to get tight with anyone in any situation. During World War I, he demonstrated again and again his knack for instantly gaining a rapport with the fighting troops by being with them at the front, getting out front when the fighting started, and saying the right thing at the right time. MacArthur was the chief of staff of the 42nd Infantry Division when the unit got over to France, and normally a chief of staff stayed in the rear running the divisional headquarters.

But even then, MacArthur was able to get capable subordinates to keep things humming in the rear while he went up front where the action was, and where MacArthur was often the focus of the action. MacArthur didn't just show up at the front; he went out of his way to connect with the troops, and the soldiers loved it. Mac-Arthur was one of the few high-ranking officers in that war who mixed it up with the soldiers while the shooting was going on. At the end of the war, men of his division chipped in and gave him a gold lighter inscribed, "To the Bravest of the Brave." It wasn't just being brave that impressed them, but being brave among the troops. In later years, MacArthur continued to touch the lives of individual soldiers. It was more difficult to do this as he achieved higher rank, for there were more and more troops under his command, and his common-touch efforts were very diluted. This is still a much-used technique of executives. Nothing like getting down in the trenches to find out what is really going on.

★ Practicing innovation. MacArthur not only encouraged new technology, but new thinking in every aspect of making war. It was easy to sell MacArthur on innovative ideas, and he was often far ahead of his younger subordinates in this respect. His troops performed more amphibious landings in the Pacific than the navy and did so in a greater variety of ways and often using more innovative techniques. This use of innovation by MacArthur often gets overlooked, partly because he was an "old man" (in his sixties) during World War II. But MacArthur was always young and smart, no matter how old he was. MacArthur proved that age is no absolute barrier to innovation. He kept on his toes mentally until he died, which proves again that if one uses it, one won't lose it.

★ Seeing the big picture. MacArthur thought big. Not just about his career, but in terms of any situation he was dealing with. Early in his career he saw that as the need to be noticed by the most senior people in the army. He was then one of thousands of lieutenants, and he realized that the handful of generals running the army could jump-start his career if they came to recognize Lieutenant Mac-Arthur. Being the son of a senior general and Civil War hero didn't hurt, but MacArthur had to do some noticeable things to get the attention his career needed, and he got himself on the fast track. When America got into World War I, MacArthur again saw the big picture. Divisions were being raised by having state National Guard units transferred to federal service. This took a while, because some state units were in better shape than others. Rather than wait for many states to get a division's worth of units together, MacArthur suggested a "Rainbow" division with troops from many states. This unit could be sent off to France more quickly, and MacArthur arranged to go as the division's chief of staff. The raising of this division became something of a media event, and MacArthur was right in the middle of it. He not only saw the big picture here, but took advantage of it on several levels. Between the World Wars, he held increasingly senior positions where he was expected to see the big picture, and he did so with more clarity than many desired. As superintendent of West Point, he saw that the decades-old instructional methods had not kept up with the needs of the twentieth century. He saw West Point as a university-level school, while the faculty saw it as a nineteenth-century military school that didn't even issue college degrees. MacArthur was correct, but he had a hard time changing things. He did, for example, introduce the awarding of bachelor degrees to graduates, instead of the nineteenth-century certificate. Later, as chief of staff of the army in the early 1930s, MacArthur saw the coming of World War II and fought vigorously to get money for the army. He was particularly keen on putting most of that money into training his soldiers. Politicians wanted him to buy weapons instead, but MacArthur knew that military technology in the 1930s was changing so fast that any new stuff would be obsolete in a few years. During World War II and into the occupation of Japan and the Korean War MacArthur demonstrated an unfailing ability to see the big picture. His vision never failed him. He may have been insufferable, but he was usually right.

★ Looking good in uniform. MacArthur was a handsome devil and filled out a uniform quite nicely. Despite his reputation for aloofness, he was quite fond of women and used his ample charm to further his amorous adventures. His pleasant appearance was used to achieve dominance in personal situations. From early in his career, he would make modifications in his uniforms so that he made even more of an impression. His handsome face was enhanced by deliberate use of facial gestures to intensify the image he was trying to project. Even posture was used. Although only five feet ten inches in height, MacArthur stood up straight, quite literally making himself appear taller than he actually was. All of this was another example of MacArthur making use of all he had in order to achieve his goals.

★ Being fearless. Although MacArthur acquired the nickname "Dugout Doug" early in World War II, he was actually quite fearless. The World War II business was produced by people in the media who didn't like MacArthur and who interpreted his departure from the Philippines in a sinister light. The story went that while in the Philippines, MacArthur cowered in a dugout (a large tunnel, actually) while his nearby troops fought it out with the Japanese. Quite untrue, but that's how it goes with spreading rumors in the press. Actually, MacArthur was his usual fearless self during the time he was on Corregidor. While the troops stayed in the massive tunnel inside the island, MacArthur continued to use his office topside. When a Japanese air raid arrived, he would, if the action was particularly hot, go jump into a slit trench. Throughout his career, MacArthur never hesitated to expose himself to enemy fire, much to the consternation of those around him. He was the most decorated U.S. Army officer in history, garnering over a dozen decorations for courage under fire.

MacArthur made mistakes, despite his ample talents. There were only a few major ones, despite his half century of military service. Each of these errors is instructive.

★ Trying to coast on his talent. Before World War I, MacArthur had a series of pretty dull assignments. With no war going on and being a lowly lieutenant of vast talents, MacArthur got sloppy. At one point he was spending so much time pursuing a love affair that it got noticed by his commanding officer. This resulted in a negative evaluation, the kind of thing that could ruin a career that was just getting started. MacArthur quickly recovered and wrote a valuable and respected manual on military demolition. That, and a generally more dedicated demeanor, kept his career on track until he could strut his stuff on the battlefield during World War I.

★ Dealing with the bonus marchers in 1932. This incident, more than any other, turned many in the media, and Americans in general, against MacArthur. The Great Depression (1929–1941) caused a movement to get a World War I veterans' bonus paid out earlier. In 1932, thousands marched on Washington, D.C., demanding that a law be passed to allow immediate payment of the bonus. MacArthur carried out his orders to remove the marchers from Washington, and the press ripped him apart. Had MacArthur used his media savvy to "control the story" better, he might have reduced the damage to his reputation. As it was, MacArthur took a lot of hits from false accusations, many of which dog his reputation to this day.

★ Preparing the Philippines for the Japanese invasion in 1941. When the Japanese invasion did come in December 1941, MacArthur was as ready as was possible. But MacArthur was also in an impossible situation. Japan's fleet and land-based bombers ruled the seas in the western Pacific. MacArthur was guaranteed to be cut off from reinforcement or resupply. He was doomed, no matter what he did. Yet MacArthur did make some mistakes, and his enemies spilled much ink turning these mistakes into major catastrophes. MacArthur did more things right than wrong during the Philippines campaign. But he did enough things wrong to give his enemies plausible grounds for calling the campaign a MacArthur-induced disaster. It was hardly that, for the Philippines were the most difficult conquest for the Japanese during their initial invasions of the war. No other Allied army held off the Japanese longer than did MacArthur's troops in the Philippines.

★ Assessing the chances of the Chinese entering the Korean War was his most notable failure. After crushing the North Korean army in the (September 1950) landing deep in their rear at Inchon, Mac-Arthur proceeded to overrun North Korea. The new Communist government in China warned that an American takeover of North Korea would result in Chinese intervention. MacArthur would not believe it, even when the evidence piled up. The Chinese forces caught MacArthur's troops unprepared for a major offensive and the U.N. forces took a major beating. Apparently MacArthur used his vast experience in the Orient to conclude that the Chinese Communists would not dare take on U.S. forces. That was a reasonable call, given the civil war the Chinese Communists had just finished winning at great cost to China. But MacArthur also thought the Chinese were indulging in the same kind of deception that the Japanese had used so often during World War II. This was not true. What evidence MacArthur saw of massive Chinese presence in Korea was not a deception, but evidence. It was an error that forever blemished an otherwise brilliant military reputation. And it's also a lesson to anyone who would rely too much on past experience.

One of the most contentious aspects of MacArthur's career was whether or not he was as good as his partisans say he was. According to many of his contemporaries, he was. British prime minister Winston Churchill called MacArthur "the glorious commander," among other flattering things. British general Bernard Montgomery stated that Mac-Arthur was America's "best soldier." British leader Lord Alanbrooke thought MacArthur was "the greatest general and the best strategist that the war produced." U.S. Army Chief of Staff General George Marshall called MacArthur "our most brilliant general." President Roosevelt had nothing but praise for MacArthur, and also thought well enough of him before the war to keep him as army chief of staff in 1933, even though MacArthur had been appointed by Roosevelt's Republican predecessor and the custom was for a new president to appoint his own man.

There has grown up a conventional wisdom regarding MacArthur that defies logic. He is accused of not caring about his troops and getting them killed unnecessarily. This was hardly the case, and Mac-Arthur had the best record of any World War II general in protecting his troops from death and injury. More American troops were killed and injured in one European theater battle (the Battle of the Bulge, in late 1944) than in all of MacArthur's Pacific battles. The Battle of the Bulge raises another interesting point. This battle was the result of Allied generals' ignoring German preparations for an offensive because, "it did not make any sense for the Germans to attack." MacArthur did the same thing in Korea and was forever slammed for it. No such fate befell Eisenhower and company for their identical gaffe in Europe. Moreover, MacArthur lost far fewer troops after his error than Eisenhower did in the Battle of the Bulge. In fact, during MacArthur's entire period of commanding the Korean War troops, he suffered only thirteen thousand casualties. One marine battle in the Pacific, the struggle for Iwo Jima, saw twice as many U.S. losses.

MacArthur was not only a very successful general, he was able to be one with uncharacteristically low casualties. Then again, as was mentioned at the beginning of this chapter, never argue with someone who buys ink by the barrel.

CHAPTER 12

★ GEORGE PATTON ★

THE TASKMASTER

THE IMAGE OF George S. Patton for most Americans is that of the movie actor George C. Scott standing in front of the American flag, ivory-handled revolvers strapped to his side, spouting hyperbole about war in the movie *Patton*. This image hides the true man. One major mistake of the movie was that Patton did not have the impressive deep baritone of George C. Scott, but a high, squeaky voice. Yes, Patton was a unique individual but he was more than the "Old Blood and Guts" (a term Patton hated) of the movie. He was probably one of the greatest captains of history and most likely the greatest battlefield commander America has produced or will ever produce. Contrary to his public image, Patton was a man of detail, given to deep thought, highly religious, a poet, and perhaps one of the best military scholars to hold the rank of general. The flamboyance was an image. This was an image Patton created in the belief that it would get men to perform the harsh task of taking lives at great risk to their own.

THE WORLD OF GEORGE PATTON (1885–1945)

Patton's world was one of ever-changing scenery. Born fifteen years before the turn of the century, George Patton was destined to see the world grow and change with unprecedented rapidity. The world would move from peace to war and back with no influence from Patton, something that would have frustrated the Great Captains of the past. The great generals before the eighteenth century often chose when and where they would fight. These choices would be made by others during Patton's career.

Patton was destined to become a military leader. He came from a long line of military men. His paternal grandfather had been killed in the Civil War. Other ancestors had served at various times and places. His own father had graduated from the Virginia Military Institute but chose not to pursue a career in the army. The senior Patton seems to have regretted the decision and instilled in his son a love for history and the armed forces.

An interesting fact that is well-known to historians, but not the general public, is that Patton was dyslexic (natural inability to read). This problem would haunt him until after his graduation from West Point. At the time this problem was not well understood. Fortunately for Patton his parents had enormous patience and great hopes for their son. His father and family made up for the dyslexia by reading to him as he grew. Eventually, he was able to overcome his disability. There were two side effects that proved positive. The first was that Patton developed an amazing memory. This would lead to his ability to keep track of a large number of details. The other side effect was that it developed Patton's tenacity. There was nothing that Patton did not feel he could train himself to understand or do. He kept at a task until he mastered it, no matter how difficult or hard. These traits would serve him well in the years to come.

Patton began his army career by seeking a West Point appointment. At first he was unsuccessful and went to the Virginia Military Institute, where many Pattons had gone before him. After spending a year at VMI, Patton won a position at West Point. It was at West Point that the young Patton began to develop his formidable attention to detail. Rarely, if ever, did the young cadet receive demerits for his appearance. While at West Point he did suffer one setback in his career. Patton was unable to pass his math exam and was held back to repeat his first year at West Point. This was surely a result of his dyslexia. After finishing his "second" first year, Patton was promoted to second corporal. Disappointed that he had not made first corporal, he consoled himself with being among the top cadets. When his senior year finally arrived Patton was appointed adjutant of the corps of cadets. Now, he was truly at the top.

After graduating from West Point in 1909, Patton chose a career in the cavalry. The army of 1909 was more similar to the armies of the Civil War than it was to the army that Patton would lead into battle thirty-five years latter. Cavalry was still seen as the arm of decision in 1909. It wasn't, but no one realized that yet.

The army in 1909 was not the vast array that would be assembled for World War I or World War II. It was scattered over numerous tiny posts in the Midwest and West. These bases were leftovers from the recently ended Indian wars. There were a few major military installations in the East. The army of this period was small, only eighty-four thousand men, a mere handful by today's standards. This meant that a young officer could remain stuck in his lowly rank for years with no hope of promotion. This was a serious impediment for someone as ambitious as George S. Patton, Jr.

Twentieth-century technology had not yet begun its transformation of the military. The army had just started to experiment with aircraft in hopes of using them for scouting, sort of a mobile balloon. No one had even thought of the tank, let alone mechanized units. These were the last days of the horse.

Patton's first exposure to action came during the 1914 feud with Pancho Villa on the Mexican border. Patton was stationed at Fort Bliss, Texas. The commanding officer there was "Black Jack" Pershing. Patton developed a relationship with Pershing that would be of benefit when the United States became involved in World War I. Not only did Patton find Pershing to be a good military contact, but Pershing became a role model for Patton. Pershing paid close attention to the details.

Patton would see some action during his time on the Mexican border. In one raid, Patton led his soldiers on perhaps the first mechanized attack by the United States Army. Patton and his troops drove to an enemy-held ranch by motor vehicle rather than by horse. They then had a quick but deadly shootout with a group of Villa's men and returned to Pershing's headquarters with the bodies of the enemy troops slung over their front fenders.

The next major event in Patton's life would be World War I (1914–18). The Great War had been in progress for over three years when the Americans finally joined in. At first Patton was assigned to Pershing's headquarters. George was keen, as always, to be in the middle of the action. So he looked for the opportunity to get involved somehow rather than follow events from the safety of headquarters.

Fortunately for Patton, the British and the French had just begun experimenting with a new weapon called the tank. In its simplest form, the tank was merely one or more machine guns or small cannon, riding on a cross-country tractor, surrounded by armor. Even before it was first used, the feeling was that the tank might revolutionize warfare. First, it had the firepower of artillery. Second, it had the mobility of cavalry. Lastly, it had the ability to become an instant pillbox (fortified gun position) anywhere on the field of battle. The British and French sought to exploit the tank's capabilities to start breaking through the otherwise impenetrable German fortifications. This would again allow mobility on the battlefield after three years of stalemate. The Americans saw the promise in this new weapon and quickly formed their own tank units.

The man Pershing chose to help set up the tank corps was George Patton. This should not have been surprising, as the appointment was encouraged by Patton himself. Patton would spend the rest of the war developing, training, and leading the new tank corps. The tank would bring Patton much success, but it would not make him a general before the war was over. In this George found bitter disappointment.

With World War I ended, Patton's world changed once again. Congress cut back the army to near its prewar level, around 130,000 troops. Army officers at this time were shuttled from one unimportant assignment to another. Often they were involved with mundane tasks like building squash courts and skeet ranges. It is surprising that so many of the heroes of World War II remained in the army during this time. Eisenhower, MacArthur, Marshall, Bradley, and Patton all stuck it out until the next war.

Hitler's invasion of Poland and then France broke Patton's twenty years of boredom. The invasions were led by Hitler's tank forces, and the United States suddenly was wakened from its slumber. After World War I, the United States had pretty much ignored tanks. The cavalry, infantry, and artillery continued their traditional prominence. The tank was the oddball element, a flash in the pan from the last year of the Great War (as World War I was known until World War II came along). What tanks American forces did have were relegated to being a part of the infantry with no clearly defined role. The German success proved that what Patton and his comrades had advocated since 1919, an independent tank corps, was the way to go. The United States Army began to play catch-up to the rest of the world. Patton's talents would be used to help build the new tank corps. For the next couple of years Patton would be involved in training the men he would lead into battle to crush the Germans.

The Americans would not actually fight their first action in the European theater until 1943. American forces were first used in North Africa in an invasion code-named "Torch." Patton had been training tank troops since 1940, and now he would lead them into combat. The entire invasion force was under the direction of Dwight Eisenhower, a close friend of Patton. Torch ended up being a success, as the Americans quickly overran the feeble resistance of the Vichy French. When the Americans moved their forces out to meet the Germans, Patton was not in command, having been assigned to tidy up the initial U.S. conquests.

The Americans met stiff resistance from the German Army. In the battle of Kasserine Pass (February 1943), American troops of II Corps were soundly defeated. This was a major embarrassment. Eisenhower realized that he needed success against the Germans, and he needed it quickly. Thus, Patton was assigned to revive the defeated II Corps. It was the moment he had prepared for all his life. With the usual Patton zeal, he began to re-form II Corps and within days started to dish it out to the Germans. Eventually, with Patton's help, the German Army would collapse in North Africa.

From North Africa, Patton moved to Sicily in the summer of 1943. There again, his skills would help lead to a German defeat. But it was there that Patton would also face his darkest hour. While touring the field hospitals in Sicily, Patton encountered men suffering battle fatigue. Two of these encounters resulted in Patton's losing his self-control and slapping each of the men. Word of the incidents eventually reached Eisenhower and almost resulted in Patton's getting sacked. If it had not been for Ike's faith in Patton's skill as a military leader, he surely would have been out of the war. The result was that Patton was sidelined until after the D-day invasion in June 1944.

Prior to D day, Patton was ordered to create his own Third Army. This force would go to France after the amphibious invasion had gotten ashore. This would prove to be Patton's most successful command and his last. Third Army played the major role in the breakout from the beachhead in July 1944. When the Battle of the Bulge came along in December 1944, Third Army was responsible for stopping the German breakthrough. If Patton had been given the free rein he desired, he would have perhaps beaten the Russians to Berlin. Soon, with Third Army's help, the war was over. Third Army had captured more ground and prisoners than any other Allied army in the west.

Patton's world ended just as it was changing once again. This time the wars were turning cold, and men of action and grit like Patton were becoming anomalies. Patton did experience the beginning of the cold war, and it proved to be a frustration for him. George spoke his mind, and the cold war era was not a time in which one could say what one felt. One had to be diplomatic; it would be the time of limited warfare, a concept Patton never could have accepted. Fortunately Patton died before he had to face the ignominious fate of Douglas MacArthur. An event like that would have surely killed him had a late-1945 automobile accident not done it first.

THE CHALLENGE

Patton's overwhelming desire was to become one of the Great Captains of history. But how does one do this when one is born into a democracy where the civilians choose when and where to fight. Until the end of the nineteenth century, nations were constantly at war, and there were any number of opportunities for a talented officer to rise to the top. However, Patton was born into a relatively uneventful time. If you look at Patton's career, only seven or eight years were actually spent practicing his craft. It was as if history had decided to change its modus operandi and pour out all its blood and horror into intense, brief spurts. Patton had to find ways to make himself stand out even though no conflicts existed.

Patton's second challenge was intertwined with the first. The United States had a very small cadre of professional officers. These men would be called on to lead amateurs into war. This was in sharp contrast to the officers of the armies of Alexander and Caesar, who had campaigned together for years at a time. The bulk of the men that served with Patton had only months before been clerks, farmers, or machinists. Patton's biggest challenge was how to turn such a ragtag force into a fighting machine.

THE SOLUTION

Patton developed himself while creating techniques to improve his own abilities and those who would serve under him. The techniques discussed below are among those Patton made use of.

★ Self-development. There has probably never been a military leader who spent as much time studying his craft. Patton was constantly adding to his huge library of military books. They were not just collected, but were actually read and studied. Patton's books are filled with notes and his thoughts on warfare. Not only did he study land warfare, he also studied the naval battles. He read both current military theory and the lessons of history. Patton availed himself of the opportunity to attend every military school that he possibly could. He was always aware of the next course he should be taking and tried to get himself into this training sooner than was typical for a career officer.

Beyond the normal military studies, Patton looked for other ways to train himself and excel. When the opportunity arose for him to participate in the 1912 Olympic modern pentathlon, Patton jumped at the chance. He felt that this would give him some of the notoriety he craved. The event consisted of running, swimming, fencing, pistol shooting, and horse riding. True to Patton form, he sought out the best swordsman in Europe to train him in fencing. For his efforts he would place an amazing fifth. And if he had not been so exhausted from a restless night before the pistol shoot, he might well have won a medal.

When asked to develop the American tank corps for World War I, Patton learned everything possible about tanks. He went to the British and French to learn how to drive and operate their armored vehicles. He spent hours with the Allied officers talking about tactics and studying their successes. George even took time to visit the factories where the tanks were produced. By the time he was through, there was not a facet of tanks that he did not understand.

When Patton began to realize that aircraft were going to play a vital part in the conflicts that followed World War I, he got his private pilots' license. This allowed him to see firsthand how aircraft could be used to support his ground forces.

There were three major results of Patton's self-development. The first was to allow his superiors to see that he was serious about his career and bring him into the limelight. The second result was more important and enduring. When Patton got in front of his troops he had credibility. He knew in depth what he spoke about. That type of confidence tends to carry itself over to an audience. Instinctively people could tell that this man was not just show, he also knew his stuff.

The last benefit of this self-development was that Patton rarely ran into a situation that he had not studied. For instance, during his tenure in France he attributed some of his success to understanding the road systems. He had carefully studied various campaigns in France. Also, Patton could compare and assess what tactics were needed in a specific instance because of the vast database of knowledge he had accumulated over the years. Patton would write, "Strategy and tactics do not change. Only the means of applying them are different."

★ Communication. In addition to studying, Patton wrote articles for publication. Every chance he had, he wrote on different aspects of the military. This is one of the ways that he kept his name in public view during all those years of peace. Patton's writing was a means of keeping his name and capabilities in view, while also getting his ideas into circulation. While not as energetic a self-promoter as MacArthur, Patton knew the value of maintaining a high profile. He was a good writer, and energetic in going about it.

★ Attention to detail. One of the enduring myths about Patton paints him as an impulsive cowboy. This was a legend that he himself cultivated. The truth of the matter was that most of what he did was done with great planning and deep thought. Patton wrote that "genius comes from the ability to pay attention to the smallest of details." He and his staffs spent hours planning and preparing for battle and thinking up contingencies. Patton's attention to preparation made it appear that he was moving effortlessly into an operation and gave the illusion of shooting from the hip.

The attention to detail let Patton know what was needed to accomplish a job and how far he could push his men. But Patton did not micromanage his subordinates. He knew what they were about and what they were doing so that he could coordinate their efforts efficiently. Too many leaders don't know what is going on, so their organizations duplicate effort or waste energy in activities that are leading nowhere.

Because of Patton's attention to detail, his army was more flexible. In fact, Third Army was, at times, attacking in three different directions at once. This was a feat that other generals would never contemplate, but one that Patton was able to pull off.

Any truly great leader must pay attention to the details of his organization. It is common for senior commanders to keep well above, and away from, what their troops are actually doing. Patton spent his time up front so that he could get a genuine feel for what was happening around him.

★ Training. Patton believed in having well-trained troops. He felt that the only way to ensure that men would perform well in battle was to have them well led, disciplined, and trained. Many times Patton was the one doing the training. Even as his rank increased he spent time in front of the troops during training. This created a bond that is not achievable any other way. Patton also knew the importance of training officers as well as troops.

His most challenging training assignment was preparing the American Expeditionary Forces' tank corps during World War I. Here Patton would train the same men that he would lead into battle. The men trained by him tended to trust him even more as he led them into combat. Patton repeated this drill with his troops getting them ready for North Africa campaigning and then again with Third Army before he took them to Europe.

It is a truism that one doesn't truly understand a subject until he must teach it. Patton's training of his men not only led to him bonding with them, but it also led him to a clearer understanding of those subjects he taught.

★ Leading by wandering around. Patton did not believe that a commander's place was in the rear at his headquarters. He felt that the only way to get things done was to be where the action was taking place. He was there when his men trained and he was there when his men executed.

When his tank corps entered battle in World War I, he went with them. In their first engagement he was up front, encouraging his men and inspiring them to go beyond the call of duty. Here Patton was very much like the captains of old who led their men into battle, rather than being behind pushing them.

During the training of combat units in World War II, Patton made sure he constantly appeared before his troops. He would be out in the field with them whenever he could, and he made sure that they knew he was there. He had a large entourage of military police outriders who would signal his coming by using sirens. The men loved it.

In order to get the II Corps ready for its first battle after its bitter defeat at Kasserine Pass, Patton went from one unit to the next for an entire week. He used the same noisy entrance he had used during training in the States. At each unit he would inspect the troops and talk to both the men and officers (together and separately). He instilled discipline wherever he went, much to the annoyance of many front-line troops, while letting everyone know what he expected. But the soldiers knew that Patton had their best interests at heart and this made a tremendous difference.

Especially during the battles of World War II, Patton would dash from unit to unit. He always seemed to be able to show up where there was trouble. Here was a leader that not only talked a good talk but actually got in and helped solve problems.

The way Patton handled the infamous slapping incident was a good example of his straight-ahead problem solving. He stood up in front of the men and apologized.

The more time a leader spends with his troops, the more they respect him. How can the troops get to know a leader if he doesn't spend time with them? How can troops follow a leader if he is not there to lead? Patton understood all of this clearly. And it is why he was always there in the midst of things.

★ Taking care of subordinates. The concern for the welfare of his men was always topmost in Patton's mind. It was related to his attention to detail. He knew that if he took care of his men, they would be more willing to do their duty. Patton watched out for his men in endless ways. He made sure they had proper quarters. He made sure they had proper rations. He made sure that their exploits were reported in the hometown papers. The slapping incident resulted from Patton's many visits to field hospitals. Even though he hated doing it, he felt his troops needed him there and deserved to have him there. During World War II he carried around a case of medals and would award one of them on the spot to a deserving soldier, and then take care of the paperwork latter. This gained enormous loyalty from the men. Patton realized that without the loyalty of his men, he could not accomplish much of anything. Patton wrote, "There's a great deal of talk about loyalty from the bottom to the top. Loyalty from the top down is even more necessary and is much less prevalent. One of the most frequently noted characteristics of great men who have remained great is loyalty to their subordinates."

★ Personality. Patton was really two men. Patton literally created the flamboyant character that most of us are familiar with. He felt that there was a certain bearing that a military leader needed to have in order to command men in battle. You can actually see the difference when you look at his military pictures and those of him in normal civilian life. Patton was profane and crude in front of the men, but could host the elite of Europe in the evening.

Patton actually practiced his war face, the face that he felt he had to have in front of the men to communicate confidence and control. Deeply emotional, Patton would struggle to hide this trait his entire life. He felt expressions of emotion were not proper for a warrior. Patton had in his mind the image of what a commander ought to be and he tried to project that image. In a true sense he was an actor on the stage of history.

Patton was one of the more complex military leaders to appear on the scene in this century. He was, in the truest sense, a self-made man, and he helped to make other men. He took nothing for granted and went at things only one way, all-out. He was also flawed. He was arrogant and a bigot. One can only wonder if he had learned to think about what he said instead of saying what he thought, if he might have achieved even higher rank.

CHAPTER 13

★ NORMAN SCHWARZKOPF ★

BUILDING ALLIANCES

SUCCEEDING IN THE most highly politicized war of this century, the 1990–91 Gulf War, Schwarzkopf did most of his important work away from the troops. Dealing with many different allies, some from nations normally hostile to the United States, he brought it all together in the most spectacular victory in American military history.

In one important respect, Schwarzkopf is unique compared to the other warriors we have studied in this book. He spent relatively little time in combat, just under three years. As a general, his time in combat amounts to only a few months, and that's if you count the preparation for Desert Storm. This makes it difficult to compare him to the other great generals. One of the accomplishments that gives him the right to stand with the others, though, is that there were so few casualties during the Gulf War. Fatalities during the Gulf War were 263 for the U.S., which is amazing when you consider that 541,000 U.S. troops took part in Desert Storm. One of General Schwarzkopf's main goals throughout his military career has been to save the lives of his troops. He succeeded in Desert Storm beyond anyone's expectation.

THE WORLD OF H. NORMAN SCHWARZKOPF (1934–)

As a teenager, H. Norman Schwarzkopf lived a life of adventure and travel that would prepare him well for his career as a soldier. Norman's father graduated from West Point and served with distinction in World

War I. Schwarzkopf's father founded the New Jersey State Police, was involved in the Lindbergh kidnapping case, and was the host for the radio show *Gangbusters* (a show much like today's *America's Most Wanted*). By the time Norman began his life on August 22, 1934, his father had established a hefty example to live up to.

When World War II broke out, the army was in need of officers, and the elder Schwarzkopf went back into uniform. The elder Schwarzkopf's military assignments took him to Iran. When the war was over Norman's father returned home to find Norman's mother struggling with alcoholism. To get Norman into a more stimulating environment, his father took Norman back with him to Iran in 1946. The elder Schwarzkopf had been asked to stay in the army after World War II, to work with the Iranian government because of Iran's strategic location next to the Soviet Union.

Norman got to experience the exotic nature of Iran. His father made sure that young Norman saw as much as possible while he was there. Norman's father was instrumental in building in his son a respect for other cultures, a trait that would become vital during the Gulf War.

Over the next few years the younger Schwarzkopf would live in Switzerland, Germany, and Italy as his father received different military assignments. During this time he was exposed to many cultures, and became fluent in German and French. Finally, his father decided it was time for him to return to the United States and pursue their mutual dream of his attending West Point. So, in 1950 Norman entered a private military school.

Valley Forge Military Academy was a typical military prep school. Schwarzkopf excelled in academics and sports. He played linebacker for the school football team and graduated as valedictorian. Schwarzkopf would say of his Valley Forge experience, "West Point prepared me for the military; Valley Forge prepared me for life."

Having excelled in so many ways at Valley Forge, Schwarzkopf was easily accepted into West Point and arrived during the summer of 1952. While at West Point, Schwarzkopf worked hard and concentrated on becoming the best cadet possible. By his senior year Schwarzkopf was appointed to the rank of cadet captain, the highest rank a cadet can achieve, and commander of his company. Schwarzkopf graduated in the top 10 percent of his class.

Schwarzkopf's high class ranking allowed him to choose any military branch he wished. At this time, Schwarzkopf could have entered the air force as the air force was still selecting cadets from West Point while they built their own military academy. The opportunity to enter the air force was tempting. The air force received a large amount of the military budget at this time, as the U.S. began to build up its strategic nuclear capabilities. Although tempted to join the more glamorous air force, Schwarzkopf decided to stay with the army. More important yet, he decided to become an infantry officer, a position that was seen as dangerous and dirty, but a path that could lead to the highest ranks. Schwarzkopf saw it as a challenge, an opportunity to be at the heart of the army and to make an impact. Schwarzkopf became so excited about the infantry that he tried to convince many of his friends to join that branch. Schwarzkopf left West Point in 1956 determined to do his best and make a difference.

The next few years were filled with the usual duties and training for a young infantry officer. From 1962–64 Schwarzkopf attended the University of Southern California to get his master's degree in mechanical and aerospace engineering, so that he could teach at West Point. This was a typical plum assignment for young officers. Beginning in 1965 he taught at West Point, but was not comfortable with it, as he saw the Vietnam War heating up. His term at West Point was supposed to last three years, but Schwarzkopf felt he had to go where the action was. Vietnam was what he, as an infantryman, had been trained for.

The army sent him to Vietnam for a year with the understanding he would return to West Point and teach for two more years. During his year in Vietnam, Schwarzkopf was a field advisor to a South Vietnamese airborne unit. Schwarzkopf then returned to teach at West Point. He felt good about his effort and experiences in Vietnam, and was surprised that he was not more warmly welcomed on his return to the States.

In 1968, Norman completed his duties at West Point. While teaching, he met and married Brenda Hoslinger, a young flight attendant.

Just before he left West Point, the army promoted Schwarzkopf to lieutenant colonel and sent him to the Command and General Staff College. This was his first step in becoming a general officer.

After completing this stint in school, Schwarzkopf volunteered for another tour in Vietnam. The Vietnam of 1969 was not the same Vietnam that Schwarzkopf had left in 1965. Cynicism had set in. Officers used tours in Vietnam merely to punch their tickets (obtain "experience" to enhance their careers). But the thirty-two-year-old lieutenant colonel did everything possible to lead his men as he felt they should be led. He fought as if the war could be won and did the best to protect the lives of his men. But all around him Schwarzkopf saw hypocrisy. The army was no longer the glamorous and romantic occupation of his youth. He returned from Vietnam disillusioned. Schwarzkopf struggled with his feeling and thought about leaving the army. He finally decided to stay and try to make things better.

For the next twenty years, Schwarzkopf's career followed the usual military pattern for an officer of his generation. During this time he had several stints at the Pentagon. But his favorite assignments where when he commanded troops. He led men in Alaska, at Fort Lewis, Washington, in Europe, and at Fort Stewart, Georgia. He commanded a brigade, a division, and finally a corps.

In 1983 Schwarzkopf became involved in operation "Urgent Fury," the invasion of Grenada. The army assigned him to be the liaison between army and naval forces. He worked side by side with the overall commander of the operation, Vice Admiral Joseph Metcalf. Grenada was the first U.S. military action since the failure of Vietnam that was a success. Schwarzkopf's advice was an important part of that success. Although the Grenada operation was a victory, there were many mistakes. Schwarzkopf noted all the mistakes and contemplated how to correct them.

In 1988 he would receive his most important command, Commander in Chief (CINC) of Central Command. Just prior to this command, Schwarzkopf had received his fourth star. Central Command (CentCom) is responsible for the Middle East. It is an interesting command in that no troops report directly to it, and it is not located in the Middle East, but in Tampa, Florida. As events take place in the Middle East, forces are assigned to CentCom. The CentCom staff was made up of three hundred staff officers from the army, navy, air force, and marines.

It appeared that the last three years of Schwarzkopf's army career would be uneventful. At the time he took over, things in the Middle East were calm. Then, in August of 1990, Iraq invaded Kuwait and changed Schwarzkopft's life. CentCom was ordered to protect Saudi Arabia from invasion.

Schwarzkopf oversaw the buildup of U.S. Persian Gulf manpower from practically nothing to a force of over 541,000 troops inside Saudi Arabia. Iraq had an equal number of troops inside of Kuwait. Normally, an attacking force needs three to one odds to defeat a defending force. Because of Schwarzkopf's brilliant planning and the fact that he was commanding the best-trained, most highly motivated, and best-equipped soldiers the United States has ever fielded in peacetime, he was able to beat the odds and pull off one of the most decisive victories in history.

THE CHALLENGE

Besides fighting in the Vietnam War, H. Norman Schwarzkopf faced two major challenges during his career. The first challenge was how to help rebuild the army after the Vietnam War disaster. The second challenge was how to defeat Saddam Hussein.

At the end of the Vietnam War, U.S. armed forces were a mess. Both the officer corps and the troops had become cynical. The ranks were filled with alcoholics, drug abusers, and kids enlisting not out of a sense of duty, but because no other jobs were available. Conscription had ended, and it was tough getting decent volunteers. The American public had lost their respect for those serving in the military. The U.S. Congress was intent on cutting the bloated military budget. It seemed as if everyone wanted to sweep the armed forces under the carpet and forget about it. An officer who desired to serve in the military of the 1970s had many problems to overcome. Schwarzkopf would rise to the challenge and do his part to rebuild the army that he would lead into war in 1991.

The challenges of the Gulf War were many and diverse, but three especially stand out. One major challenge was coordinating the multinational forces which were brought to bear against Saddam. The coalition would consist of thirty-three countries. Many of these countries were from the Middle East and were easily offended but vital to the political success of the mission. Another major challenge of the Gulf War was the motivation of the troops. The desert is a boring place. The problem is how to keep the troops motivated for weeks on end. The last major challenge that Schwarzkopf faced was how could he attack the fourth largest army in the world, considered by many to be quite formidable, and keep his casualties to a minimum.

THE SOLUTION

Schwarzkopf mustered his own collection of solutions. This was his bag of tricks, and it was similar to what the other Great Captains had used throughout history.

★ The soldiers come first. Schwarzkopf cared deeply about the soldiers who served under him. One of the ironies of the Gulf War was that Dan Rather of CBS News accused Stormin' Norman of not caring enough for his troops. Everyone who knew him knew that Schwarzkopf lived and died for the common infantry soldier. They thought it humorous, and at the same time galling, that Rather would attempt to lecture the general on how to care for his troops.

Schwarzkopf looked up to commanders who had respect for their troops. One of his heroes was the Civil War general William Tecumseh Sherman. Sherman had a deep and abiding respect for the common soldier. Another general that Schwarzkopf looked up to was one of his own commanders, Major General Richard Cavazos. Schwarzkopf served under Cavazos while commanding an infantry brigade at Fort Lewis, Washington, in 1977. Cavazos was a Korean War veteran who, in the words of Schwarzkopf, "was a great commander of troops." One way that Cavazos showed his own caring for his troops was challenging any activity that would force his troops to work on the weekend. Schwarzkopf followed this example to the point that he did not have a victory parade immediately on his return from the Gulf War, as it would have had to be held on Sunday. This is not a trivial act by a commander. Combat units often do have to work on weekends, especially when they are out on field exercises.

An example of Schwarzkopf's concern for the troops occurred early on in his career. In 1965, during his first tour in Vietnam, he advised a group of Vietnamese soldiers not to participate in a battle because there was not enough artillery and air support. The Vietnamese commanding officers were furious. Schwarzkopf didn't care. He felt his first responsibility was to the lives of his troops.

The concern for the troops extended to their families. As he rose in rank Schwarzkopf looked for ways to help the families of the soldiers and make their lives more comfortable. He sponsored family days in the units he commanded, and his wife Brenda became active with the army communities where they were stationed.

Schwarzkopf's feeling for his soldiers is illustrated in his words as he left the 24th Infantry Division, which he commanded from 1983 to 1985. His parting words were, "I've loved you as only a soldier can love a soldier." This type of caring motivated troops in training during the seventies and eighties and motivated the troops to perform at high levels during the Gulf War.

★ Passion. Schwarzkopf's passions run deep and he is well-known for his temper. This can be seen in his two nicknames, "Bear" and "Stormin' Norman." The first nickname can be used to his face. The second one is usually used when he is not in the room. This passion kept him at a task when most people would have given up.

One might be tempted to call Schwarzkopf's passion commitment, but it is more than that. His passion for what is right lets him speak out about things that he thinks are wrong. For instance, early during Desert Shield, the White House asked him to prepare a plan for trying to dislodge the Iraqis when the American forces only numbered about two hundred thousand. The general and his staff felt that to try to attack the Iraqis at that time would have been a mistake. Schwarzkopf and his staffed prepared a plan as requested. But Schwarzkopf made sure the White House knew why the plan would not work. He held nothing back in his description of what would happen if the plan was attempted, especially the large number of American casualties. The White House never asked for the plan to be implemented. One wonders what would have happened if the U.S. forces had not been led by such a passionate leader. Would the U.S. have attacked too soon and suffered painful losses, and possibly even defeat?

Schwarzkopf's passion caused him to lose his temper at times. He became mad at things and situations, but rarely at his own people. This is an important distinction if a commander wants people to keep following him. If Schwarzkopf ever felt that he had become too angry, or that he had hurt someone during his outbursts, he would apologize.

★ Respect for other cultures. Early in his life Schwarzkopf was taught to respect other cultures. While in Iran with his father, he was given many practical examples. While on a trip into the desert with his father, they stopped at the camp of one of the nomadic tribes. The chief of the tribe honored them with a dinner that evening. One way of showing honor to guests was to serve them the eyes of the sheep that had been slaughtered for the feast. First, Schwarzkopf's father was offered an eye, and then the younger Schwarzkopf himself was offered the other. Schwarzkopf knew that if he did not eat the eye his father would be disappointed and that the tribe would be offended. He screwed up all the courage that a twelve-year-old boy could and gulped down the eye, pleasing his father and the locals.

While an advisor on his first tour in Vietnam, Schwarzkopf lived like his Vietnamese counterparts. He ate the same food they did, slept in the same places, and tried to share in their lives as much as possible. This made him one of the most well accepted advisors in the country.

All of this training and experience paid off in the Gulf War. At first the allies were concerned about whether this man, with a reputation for being outspoken, could work with all the different countries involved in the conflict. But because of Schwarzkopf's attitude toward others, he was able to hold the coalition together. Schwarzkopf was even able to win over one of the most difficult personalities of the war, Prince Khalid of Saudi Arabia. Khalid was one of the top military leaders in the Arab nations, but had the reputation for being a difficult personality. Once Schwarzkopf had won Khalid's trust, many difficulties were overcome as if by magic.

Because Schwarzkopf had a deep respect for other cultures, he made sure his soldiers respected the customs of Saudi Arabia. Almost without exception the soldiers fell into line. There could have been many cultural problems between the U.S. forces and the other allied forces, but because of the general's diplomatic skills, all the problems were overcome.

★ Solution-oriented. During his first years as a young officer, Schwarzkopf had a commanding officer who was an alcoholic. This shocked and disillusioned Schwarzkopf so much he thought about leaving the army. But he found ways to work around the problem. After the Vietnam experience, Schwarzkopf was again disaffected, which appeared to be an occupational hazard of being an idealist. Instead of giving up his military career, Schwarzkopf decided to stay in the army and try to fix things. Throughout his career Schwarzkopf would identify problems and then find solutions.

An example of his solution-oriented nature came while he was commanding the 24th Infantry Division at Fort Stewart, Georgia. It was 1983, and the army had decided to make the energy conservationists happy by forbidding any lighted Christmas decorations on military camps. Schwarzkopf was very concerned about how this would affect the morale of his troops. In true Schwarzkopf fashion he came up with a solution, and the Christmas lights burned bright at Fort Stewart that winter. Soon a phone call came from General Cavazos, Schwarzkopf's immediate superior. He questioned Schwarzkopf about the lights and Schwarzkopf unveiled his solution. Schwarzkopf had calculated the amount the electricity would cost, a little over $400, and had sent a personal check to the army for the amount. Cavazos was amused, and Schwarzkopf's troops' morale remained high.

★ Courage. The Schwarzkopf courage is renowned. An example of his nerve occurred during his second tour in Vietnam. One of the companies under his command had walked into a minefield. The commanding officer and a lieutenant were wounded. Schwarzkopf landed his helicopter beside the minefield and took charge of the situation. He knew that with the commanding officer out of action, the troops might panic and suffer more casualties. As Schwarzkopf tried to talk the men out of the minefield, another mine went off, severely wounding one of the soldiers. The man began to thrash around. Schwarzkopf was afraid that he would set off yet another land mine. So he walked into the minefield and toward the wounded soldier. Schwarzkopf immobilized the thrashing trooper by pressing him to the ground while trying to calm the man down. While getting everyone out of the minefield, another officer was wounded and another soldier killed. Amazingly, Schwarzkopf's heroic act of walking into the minefield just the way he did had probably saved his own life. Many more soldiers could have died that day if it had not been for Schwarzkopf's courage. This is the type of courage that the "Bear" exhibited in all his activities. It let him speak his mind when other officers would have held their tongues. It let his troops know that he would do the right thing. It let him speak his mind about the premature plan to attack Kuwait that could have cost so many lives.

★ Communication. Schwarzkopf is a master of spoken communication. It is a talent he began to develop in high school, where he was a master debater. Whenever possible, he would stand in front of his troops and speak. He became famous at Fort Stewart for his "Carve a V" speeches. These were speeches where he would tell the troops that he would carve a 'V,' the symbol of the 24th Infantry, in the chest of their defeated enemies. The troops loved the down-to-earth nature expressed when he spoke to them.

Examples of Schwarzkopf's communication skills appeared during the Gulf War in his now famous briefings. What made these briefings so well received was their directness, simplicity, and truthfulness, laced with Schwarzkopf's own unique style of humor. This simplicity and matter-of-fact manner were present in all of his communications. Schwarzkopf was the same whether he spoke to subordinates, superiors, or the press.

One mistake Schwarzkopf recognized during the Vietnam War

and the Grenada operation was the failure to communicate effectively with the press. Schwarzkopf went to extraordinary lengths to make sure the press was informed of what was happening during the Gulf War. Doing press conferences himself was an idea that paid dividends over and over again. Schwarzkopf realized that if he did not tell the story himself, someone else would, and they would probably tell it in a way he would not like. Schwarzkopf was always direct. If he did not want to answer a question or did not have the answer, he never invented something. He would simply say he was not going to answer the question, or that he did not have the answer. Leaders who try to be clever and fool the press, or public, only end up getting caught and coming across as insincere; Schwarzkopf understood this.

★ Training. Schwarzkopf emphasized training whenever he was in direct command of troops. He trained his troops harder and longer than most commanders. During the Gulf War he trained the troops constantly. Schwarzkopf realized that there were two purposes in training. First, it kept his troops sharp and prepared for whatever would be thrown at them. Second, it kept the troops from becoming bored and worrying about home. Schwarzkopf intuitively realized that hard training, rather than destroying morale, builds it. The more the troops trained, the more confident they became, and the more confident they became, the higher their morale.

Schwarzkopf is an excellent mentor. When commanding other officers he would look for opportunities to put his arm around them and explain how things were to be done. He would take any opportunity presented to instill his leadership principles in younger officers.

★ Leading by example. One of Schwarzkopf's heroes was Alexander the Great. Alexander made an impression on Schwarzkopf because everything that Alexander's troops could do, Alexander could do better. Schwarzkopf set Alexander's example as his goal. During his tours in Vietnam he got out front with the troops as much as possible. While commanding peacetime troops he would often participate in the same activities: going on marches with them, eating

›

the same food, and so on. When the troops had to spend their Christmas away from their families during the Gulf War, Schwarzkopf did the same. It would have been easy for Schwarzkopf to have gotten on a plane and flown home. It also would have been a mistake, and Schwarzkopf knew it.

★ Understanding the enemy. Schwarzkopf spent a lot of time thinking about his enemy in the Gulf War. His first rule was not to underestimate Saddam's capabilities. He preached this to everyone. Schwarzkopf was facing a force that was well equipped and capable of doing a lot of damage. One mistake, one miscalculation, could cost hundreds of friendly lives. This was Schwarzkopf's waking nightmare. He was not going to underestimate the enemy as so many failed generals of the past had. Schwarzkopf also kept track of what the Iraqis were doing. Every day he spent hours poring over maps, reading intelligence reports, and trying to figure out what Saddam and his generals were doing. A troop movement here, a fragmentary radio message there, could speak volumes to Schwarzkopf and his staff. Schwarzkopf also analyzed Saddam to figure out what the Iraqi leader might expect in different situations. Schwarzkopf felt that one of Saddam's biggest flaws was that he expected the Americans to fight the Gulf War like they had fought the Vietnam War. Saddam was in for a big surprise because across the line in the desert were a general and an army that were going to do everything possible not to fight the Gulf War in any way like the Vietnam War.

★ Planning. The now famous "Hail Mary" plan (going deep into the desert to outflank the Iraqis) was one of the best-thought-out and executed plans in American military history. Schwarzkopf, an amateur magician, saw an opportunity to pull off a spectacular act of misdirection. This was a magician's technique, where he says, "look here," while the real action takes place somewhere else. For his "Hail Mary" maneuver to succeed, there were three parts to the plan that had to be executed to perfection. First, the coalition air forces had to distract and blind the Iraqi forces. They did this by flying more sorties (a sortie is one plane flying a mission) in a matter of days than any air force of a similar size had done in the past. The second part of the plan was that Schwarzkopf had to convince the Iraqis he was coming in through the front door, right up the coast and into the Iraqi fortified line. He did this by placing his forces up against coast on the Kuwaiti border and having a large force of marines off the coast. The final piece of the misdirection was to move more than half his forces deep into the desert, where they could then perform a large flanking movement into the rear of the Iraqi forces occupying Kuwait. The trick was not to let Saddam know that these troops (we're talking about over fifty thousand vehicles) were moving to the western desert. In order for the last piece to be successful, the first two pieces had to work.

Because of the immense amount of planning that went on, the coalition forces were able to pull off the misdirection, and the flanking maneuver succeeded with almost no problem. One reason this succeeded so well is that Schwarzkopf would not accept solutions that endangered his plan. Also, he did not try to execute his plan too soon. He requested and got permission to launch his attack only when he felt he was ready. Many leaders get excited and launch their plans prematurely; this was not the case with Schwarzkopf.

★ Role models. All through his life, Schwarzkopf chose role models to learn from. His first and most important role model was his father. His father taught him duty and honor long before West Point did. His father also taught him about the importance of family and the importance of respecting other people's culture and beliefs.

His role models at the beginning of his career were Alexander the Great, William Tecumseh Sherman, and Ulysses S. Grant. He felt that these were leaders who were what he calls "muddy boot" leaders. These are the kinds of leaders who get out with the troops and lead by example. Later he would find role models under whom he served. Creighton Abrams, a former armor commander during World War II, and a favorite of Patton, led the troops during the closing years of Vietnam. Schwarzkopf felt that Abrams had kept his humility and humanity about him as he became the number one general in the army. At the end of the his career he began to look to men like Albert Schweitzer and Chief Joseph of the Nez Percé. Schwarzkopf realized early that there was much to learn from others and has continued learning throughout his life.

★ Well-rounded. Schwarzkopf was such a successful leader because he is so well-rounded. Schwarzkopf loves the outdoors and outdoor activities; he shoots trap and is interested in most sports. On the more erudite side, he listens to opera, reads military history and natural history. And as mentioned before, Schwarzkopf is an amateur magician. To Schwarzkopf, family is all-important, and he is a very spiritual man. A Bible lay by his bed throughout the Gulf War and was well read. His interest in many different things allowed him to think about problems in many different ways, sometimes coming up with very original solutions. His family and spiritual values allowed him to keep things in perspective.

All of Schwarzkopf's actions come back to two things: the soldier comes first, and doing what is right. These seem to be the two governing principles that enabled an American officer a year away from retirement to win one of the most spectacular victories of the twentieth century. Could any other American general have accomplished as much in the Gulf War? Perhaps. We'll never know. But in this case, Norman Schwarzkopf was in the right place at the right time. He had what was needed to get the job done. That's all that was required.

CHAPTER 14

TIMELESS TECHNIQUES FOR
WAR AND PEACE

WRITING IN A letter to his son, George Patton noted that leadership is what wins battles. "I have it, but I'll be damned if I can define it." From Alexander of Macedon to Norman Schwarzkopf, each of the Great Captains "has it." Leadership is a difficult concept to define, for it includes a wide array of capabilities that can be used in endless combinations. But if a general or manager can lead, all else becomes possible. In this chapter we explore the collected techniques the Great Captains used to achieve that elusive quality of leadership.

The Great Captains were all different personalities, each with a unique collection of skills. Our Great Captains also faced different times and different situations. Each of the Great Captains used different techniques to achieve his success. One thing they all had in common was the ability to mobilize their skills into a successful style of leadership. Modern managers face much the same situation. As a manager, you must lead, and the only way you can do that is to use your innate skills as effectively as possible.

We have identified dozens of different techniques, skills, and characteristics that they used. Here we suggest how you can apply them personally. The experiences of the Great Captains, if mastered by today's managers, will make them the great managers of tomorrow.

The lessons of the Great Captains are time-tested and indisputably effective.

Observe, digest, and learn.

COMMUNICATION

Communication is the key for getting anything done. Have you ever seen an effective leader who could not communicate? Leaders who fail to communicate fail. If there is any one skill that all Great Captains use, and use to greatest effect, it is communication.

The Great Captains were all excellent, or at least adequate, communicators. Managers must be able to communicate to several different groups: subordinates, superiors, peers, strategic partners, the press, and the competition. All of our Great Captains were adept at both writing and speaking to many different audiences. The same is true for today's successful managers.

The Great Captains used a wide variety of communication techniques. When communicating with any group, the Great Captains tried to be clear and precise. There was a constant danger of messages being misunderstood, resulting in disaster. Military history is littered with situations where a commander did not get the message delivered to the right person at the right time. More disastrous were the messages that were poorly written and misinterpreted to catastrophic effect. Mistakes like these are made every day in the business world, causing enormous losses as employees pursue wrong paths, strategic alliances become confused, and the wrong messages about companies are communicated via mass media.

While most of the Great Captains' communication advantage was in sending clear messages to subordinates, allies, and the general public, others went even farther. Alexander, Edward III, Napoleon, and Mac-Arthur were masters of propaganda and public relations. Considering that all but one of these men operated before the advent of mass media, one can appreciate how important this talent is. Indeed, the development of mass media has made public relations an even more powerful tool for generals and executives. The American military learned all about this the hard way during the Vietnam War (1964–1972). Although U.S. generals had been sparring with the mass media since the 1860s, they underestimated the ever-growing power of the media as they entered the television age. Vietnam was the first televised war, and the military found itself groping for adequate ways to communicate with the public and its civilian leadership. The fact that Vietnam was an unpopular war didn't help, but the sheer power mass media now had over public opinion was something the military didn't get a handle on until the 1980s. In the past, however, the Great Captains were exceptional in that they saw first the possibilities available in the media of their day. Alas, there were no American Great Captains available during the Vietnam War. In fact, the North Vietnamese demonstrated a better grasp of how to use the media. This was largely because the Communists and Fascists of the early twentieth century got as far as they did in no small measure because they better understood how to use the mass media to mobilize, mold, and manipulate public opinion. Business saw the communication potential of mass media from the beginning, and thus we have advertising and public relations (PR) as an industry. But it was only early in this century that the PR angle was developed. The military in some nations, such as the U.S., adopted civilian public-relations techniques. But only a few individuals, like MacArthur, Patton, and the entire U.S. Marine Corps, took full advantage of media manipulation. MacArthur found that this could be a dangerous game, largely because he had been at it for decades and picked up a lot of media enemies along the way. Most people, be they military officers or business executives, do not eagerly embrace aggressive PR techniques. The media can be scary, for the journalists and editors wield great power and are known sometimes to use it vindictively and capriciously. If one tries to manipulate the media and doesn't pull it off, the retribution can be painful, and costly. Careers can be quickly brought low by a losing encounter with the press. A casualty like this, caused by the media's paper bullets, is, in some ways, more to be feared than an encounter with real bullets. Death or injury in combat will at least get you something positive, be it a promotion or a medal. But paper bullets can destroy your life while leaving you around to contemplate your reduced circumstances. Great Captains, and those who would emulate them, must be willing to take on the media and win. There are examples of how it can be done. A recent one was Norman Schwarzkopf. Study what he did, and do as he did as best you can. And maybe better.

Another common communication tactic with the Great Captains

was taking their message directly to the troops. Too many managers make the mistake of not talking to those out on the front line. Top management is caught up in writing flowery mission statements and transmitting lists of admirable goals, but they fail to communicate on a basic level. Generals tend to do this also. But the Great Captains were often out talking directly to the troops, giving them precise instructions. The great manager is a constant communicator. How can employees be expected to do what the boss wants if the details are not adequately communicated.

Effective communication also depends on trust and discipline. Messages are expected to be accurate and, if orders, promptly acted upon. Too often, military commanders or business managers will tell a superior one thing and then go off and do something else. Soon the boss sees that he must micromanage the subordinate or, worse yet, remove him. Our Great Captains kept their superiors and peers informed. Many managers make the mistake of not talking with their subordinates and also failing to tell their peers and superiors what they are doing. This leads to confusion. Or it can lead people to think that the manager is ineffective.

When communicating with the "enemy" (the competition, strategic partners, or the press) what one does not say is as important as what one does say. It is still important that business leaders be clear and precise with these groups, but it is vital that they not tip their hand or give up too much information. Cooperation with an ally is essential, but the great managers must remember that information given to them may not always be secure. Business leaders should never tell an ally something that they don't want the enemy to know at a later time. We can see that throughout history allegiances shift. A manager who opens the kimono too far is an unwise manager.

Another way to avoid problems with communications is, as Patton demonstrated, to emphasize collecting and interpreting information about the enemy and one's allies. This is called "intelligence" in the military, and Patton was one of the best practitioners in this area. Patton's instructions to his subordinates always had the benefit of thorough intelligence work on the enemy. This ensured that the subordinates received orders that could be executed without many unpleasant surprises from the opposition. Thus Patton's orders were not received with dread, as were the orders from less well prepared commanders.

When managers deal with the mass media and the competition, their communications must be exact. The press and the enemy will make use of ambiguity to speculate on the manager's real intent. Business leaders cannot let fear of a misstep in public prevent them from communicating. Remember, if great managers don't tell their own story, someone else will. Skillful use of the mass media can help business leaders shape their image to the world and their competition. Poor use of the mass media can reveal, accurately or not, a company on its way out.

COURAGE

Our Great Captains were, as one would expect, endowed with enormous amounts of courage. It is easy to see why military leaders need to have courage; they are required to face death as part of their job. But our Great Captains had more than just courage in the conventional sense. Courage comes in many forms, and a Great Captain needs courage in decision making as well. This is what separates the merely fearless battlefield officer from the commander who dares what few others will attempt. As many commanders and executives can attest, it takes more courage to order someone to do something that one knows one could go do better oneself than to do it oneself. But this is what separates the Great Captains from the meek micromanagers. A Great Captain prepares for a battle, getting to know who can do what in his army, then has the courage of his convictions to launch his troops into the fray under many different leaders. Too many managers and generals dither and plan endlessly, lacking the courage to risk all, even if it means an opportunity to gain all. Humans, so to speak, are risk averse. We would rather risk nothing, even if the potential payoff is huge. The Great Captains have the courage to make their play. The difference between courage and rashness is another ability a Great Captain brings to the table. Put together a good plan, and then have the courage to have your subordinates carry it out, and you are in company with the Great Captains.

Courage is an important trait if you want to inspire your followers. If the Great Captains had not displayed courage, their soldiers would not have followed them. If a business leader does not have the courage to do the hard tasks, neither will the followers. Courage in the business world means standing up for what is right even though it might endanger the manager's career. It means taking risk where others won't. Courage in the workplace is exercised when facing the difficult employee before the annual review. Courage is also admitting to your subordinates that you have made a mistake.

Above all else, great managers take risks. Calculated risks, not rash ones. When subordinates see their leaders taking risks, they will be more likely to take risks. Conservative leaders breed conservative followers. Our Great Captains did not take risks just for the sake of taking risks. Sometimes managers think that taking risks is a virtue in and of itself, so they take risks when they shouldn't. The great leader knows when to take a risk and when not to. The Great Captains usually took risks in order to turn the battle around when they were losing it, or when the payback for taking the risk was greater than not taking the risk. Sometimes a risk is not a risk. Grant's ordering Sherman to march through Georgia in 1865, cut off from Union supply bases, was considered a risky military maneuver. Sherman and Grant, though, understood through experience that they were not taking as much risk as an uninformed observer might think. Sherman and Grant were correct, and the American Civil War was soon over as a result. A great manager only takes risk when he understands what can be lost and what can be gained by his actions.

Lastly, there is what we might call enthusiasm for risk. Many of the Great Captains relished situations where courageous decisions were called for. Like someone addicted to gambling, these warriors lived for the risks and exhilaration of combat. Some businesses attract the same kind of people. The financial markets are a prime example, as are most jobs that involve sales. If you have an enthusiasm for risk, and know how to calculate the risks and rewards accurately, then you have the makings of a Great Captain, or a successful manager.

PEOPLE SKILLS

The typical popular view of a military commander is an officer scream-ing into the face of a private and telling him to do push-ups. This type of toughness is sometimes required in the military. Yet the Great Cap-tains were more likely to be companionable and inspiring when around the troops. The rough stuff was left to the drill sergeants. Every effective organization has its fire-breathing "drill sergeants," but to perform at peak levels, one needs a Great Captain who can motivate from within while the drill sergeants work from without.

Great managers realize that they must be able to relate to their followers. Subordinates will not eagerly follow someone they feel does not care for them. For this reason, great leaders make an effort to spend as much time as possible with the troops because it is one way to communicate to followers that one cares for them. "Managing by wandering around" was a concept that Alexander and the other Great Captains understood before the business management world invented it.

It's not easy staying in touch with the troops. There are many bar-riers between employees and managers, or generals and soldiers. Great managers must do everything possible to get down to where the work is being done and connect with the people doing it. One gains a tremendous advantage, be it on the battlefield or in the marketplace, if your "troops" feel the boss is tuned in and out front with a winning plan. It is more common for senior people to throw up artificial bar-riers, like reserved parking spots and executive dining rooms. The Great Captains had privileges, no doubt, but the leaders who related to their troops the best shared the same conditions that their soldiers endured. Actually, the privileges issue is one of perceptions. All or-ganizations expect the boss to have some perks. But if you play down the bennies and show yourself comfortable, or at least familiar, with how your people live, you do wonders for morale.

MacArthur made his reputation in part by his fearless presence at the front, where the troops and the enemy fire were. MacArthur would regularly stand up and walk around under enemy fire. While some of the troops thought he was nuts, they all appreciated a senior commander coming up front to see for himself what was happening and to share in the dangers of combat. While some in the media tagged MacArthur as "Dugout Doug" in World War II, he continued to visit troops under fire throughout the war. And he continued to have the same effect on the soldiers, who could see for themselves that the boss was where the action was and showed no fear.

But one could not get anywhere simply making a show of knowing the troops, getting shot at, and sharing their food. One had to do tangible things. The Great Captains knew that, as Napoleon put it, "the morale is to the material as three is to one." What the individual soldier felt he was capable of made all the difference. And the troops felt a lot more enthusiastic if their physical needs were taken care of. The Great Captains took care of their troops in numerous ways. Seemingly mundane things like getting them fed regularly and ensuring that they had adequate weapons and equipment made a big difference. It also helped if one demonstrated a desire to limit casualties. MacArthur was one of the most effective commanders in this respect, developing tactics that kept the friendly losses lower than any other commander during World War II. These needs are as important today as they were twenty-five hundred years ago.

Great managers always show respect for their subordinates. The Great Captains understood that if they didn't respect their soldiers, no respect would be returned. Followers who are respected, and who have that respect communicated to them, will dig down deep and serve the leader more loyally than a subordinate who performs out of fear. This was particularly true with the Great Captains' immediate subordinates. No one, be he general or squad leader, personally supervises more than a dozen people. A Great Captain must select a dozen men who will in turn select their dozen subordinates all the way down to the leader of ten or so soldiers in the ranks. No one can become a Great Captain if he cannot select outstanding subordinates. In modern armies, huge bureaucracies in themselves, a general does not always have the ability to select his immediate subordinates. But this becomes yet another challenge, forcing the commander to make the best of what is made available. A Great Captain always finds a way to make the most of his people skills.

The Great Captains all understood human nature. The great manager has to be willing to tolerate mistakes because he is working with people and not machines. The business leader needs to recognize the strengths and weaknesses of his people and maximize the strengths and minimize the weaknesses. The Great Captains, even the most seemingly pitiless, knew how to make use of their subordinates' strengths and weaknesses.

Skill at dealing with human nature pays short- and long-term dividends.

LEADING BY EXAMPLE

A characteristic that is related to people skills is leading by example. This is the most elementary of leadership skills and is almost a cliché, but should not be ignored. The Great Captains would never expect their troops to do something they themselves would not do. Every Great Captain we have studied led his troops into battle at some point in his career. Gustavus, even though he was king, also got into the trenches and dug fortifications alongside his musketeers. Managers expecting their employees to work long hours must do the same. Business leaders wanting quality work and subordinates paying attention to details should expect the same of themselves. And you've got to find ways to let your subordinates know that you practice what you preach.

In the past, the supreme leader was seen as a supreme warrior. This was literally true before the twentieth century, and is still held up as an ideal today. Ambitious military officers still go to great lengths to participate, close to the shooting, in whatever wars come along. They know, as Patton and MacArthur did, that what valiant deeds one did as a young officer would, like compound interest, grow in usefulness over the years. Not only would such early heroics help one get promoted, but tales of earlier battlefield prowess would be repeated, and often embellished, by the soldiers under one's command. If one became a general, those ancient exploits tend to make the "old man" a mighty warrior in his youth. At least in the minds of one's subordinates. This is not a bad thing, for it gives the troops an example of prowess when one was their age, and what one expects of them. Leading by example, even if some exaggeration's involved, is always a good thing. And even civilian organizations have gossip about the boss, and whether any particular executives were outrageous go-getters in their younger days. The buzz about one's past can play a large role in how enthusiastic one's current subordinates will be toward one's current leadership and future plans.

Military leaders lead by example in more prosaic ways. Modern armies comprise a large number of professional soldiers with families. Military service, with its extended trips overseas and long hours otherwise, is hard on marriages. Exceptional commanders make an extra effort to ease the strains on military families, but few use it as an opportunity to lead by example. Norman Schwarzkopf is a good example of the peacetime commander who personally got out front in this area. Schwarzkopf already had a reputation for wartime bravery, but he showed the way in sticking his neck out for military families and peacetime concerns. These problems with families are increasingly common in nonmilitary organizations. The civilian manager can, in this case, look to the military solutions for help.

Managers today, especially in large corporations, have more problems leading by example. Executives are often brought in from outside. This immediately presents morale problems, because their subordinates know that the new boss hasn't walked in their shoes. The new executive's decisions are automatically questioned because the new guy, "doesn't know what it's like." Many corporations try to overcome these problems by promoting from inside and ensuring that managers tagged for the fast track to senior positions first work in as many areas of the business as possible. Many modern armies go so far as to have officer candidates serve for a time in the ranks. The ancient Romans recruited their junior officers (centurions) from among the soldiers. This provided a corps of officers who had undisputedly "been there," and who were the most effective professional officers' corps for many centuries.

Businesses that operate in "combat (or conflict) mode" most of the time, like financial markets and sales, tend to be more keen to have executives who have proven themselves in the trenches. These firms know that without "combat-proven" leaders, the troops will be much less effective, and the results will quickly show up on the bottom line.

Thus the problem of "leading by example" is widely recognized. The solution, however, continues to be more elusive for many firms.

PLANNING AND ORGANIZATION

Many of the Great Captains were amazing organizers. Innovative and/ or thorough, they ensured that their fighting troops had what they needed when it was needed. The Hollywood view of great leaders is of the visionary, or the impetuous hero, but definitely someone who is not bogged down with details. Although vision is an important trait for a leader, and there are times when a manager needs to be impetuous, the Great Captains were primarily masters at planning and organization. This requires a leader who is aware of details. If planning is not done at a detailed level, it becomes only an outline of what a manager would like to accomplish. The Great Captains knew exactly how and what things were going to be done before they entered the battle, because they had spent enormous amounts of effort planning beforehand. The Great Captains' concepts of how to carry out their operations were not just clever ideas written on a scrap of paper, but worked out over years of careful thought.

Without proper planning, it is impossible for a manager to predict how long projects will take, what resources will be needed, or what the costs will be. Improper planning leads to projects that are late and over budget. Improper planning leads to failure. Good planning is when a leader knows where he is going and how he is going to get there. The Great Captains never took to the field of battle without a plan. Many managers, though, go through their entire careers managing by the seat of their pants, reacting instead of acting. They can get away with this if they are not competing with people who do plan. But if they run into a Great Captain in the planning department, it will ruin their day. Not to mention their careers. A good plan allows a leader to be in control of the situation instead of the situation controlling the manager. And it minimizes unpleasant surprises.

Throughout history, the Great Captains tinkered with their organizations to find the format that would be the most effective. Great managers realize the organization is the vehicle for carrying out their plans. While there is no perfect organization, a poor organization can cause confusion and result in a good plan being poorly executed. Great leaders look for organizational changes that help them execute their plans more effectively. We have historical records, going back over three thousand years, detailing what generals had to do when planning wars. Then, as now, the competent general had to concern himself with details on the weapons and equipment his troops would use and the problems of keeping his soldiers fed and healthy while living in the countryside. A well-organized army is better able to prepare its troops for battle. Many of the Great Captains came up with organizational changes that became standard for centuries afterward.

For as long as there have been wars, military leaders have realized that battles are only a small part of waging war. Behind the battles are all of the preparatory work. Supplies, ammunition, and weapons must be obtained and brought to the combat zone. Businesses also depend on superior planning and organization to accomplish better their, well, business. But in this century we have seen a proliferation of businesses, or parts of some, that don't produce anything one can touch. There are now lots of "staff people" who, to all appearances, eat resources and don't do anyone, who *is* producing, much good. From the time of the Romans to the present, the combat troops have called those easygoing folks in the rear all sorts of nasty names. These staffs have always existed to some extent, and they have always been difficult to manage and tended to grow larger at the least opportunity. Military and business leaders have both had problems with proliferating staffs. Several thousand years ago, it was the sign of a Great Captain if a leader gathered around him several dozen people who could write, count, and make themselves useful while the leader planned his campaigns. Today, a Great Captain might have thousands of people on his staffs, all getting in the way. The task then becomes one of simply getting rid of most of the staff drones while keeping the few that one needs. Whether a leader wears a uniform or a suit, this problem of "staff management" has proven a difficult one.

A notable problem in military, and to a lesser extent, civilian organizations in this century is the changing ratio of "camp followers" to "warriors." A century ago, most armies comprised over 80 percent fighters and the rest "camp followers (support troops) in uniform." Today the ratio is reversed, and therein resides a major problem.

One of the great revolutions in military operations in this century has been in the enormous increase in support troops. This after a sharp drop in the proportion of camp followers in the eighteenth and nineteenth centuries. Before that it was common for an army on the march to consist of 10 to 20 percent soldiers and the rest camp followers. There was a reason for this. Armies "in the field" were camping out, and living rough could be unhealthy and arduous if you didn't have a lot of servants along to take care of the camping equipment and help out with the chores. Generals usually had to allow a lot of camp followers in order to get the soldiers to go along with the idea of campaigning. Only the most disciplined armies could do away with all those camp followers and get the troops to do their own housekeeping. The Romans had such an army, with less than half the "troops" being camp followers. But the Romans' system was not reinvented until the eighteenth century, when many European armies trained their troops to do their own chores in the field, just as the Romans had. In the nineteenth century, steamships and railroads came along and made supplying the troops even less labor-intensive, and more dependent on civilian support "troops."

Most of the growing quantities of supplies and equipment for the troops was provided by civilians, in the form of workers who produced the weapons and other supplies back home, and then ran the ships and railroads that carried all this stuff to the troops. Gradually, as one gets closer to the fighting, more and more of the support people are in uniform, often doing the same jobs as others further back. But as a result of this trend, and the increasing use of technology, today's armies are less than 20 percent warriors and the rest "camp followers in uniform." In effect, the uniformed camp followers outnumber the fighters in the armed forces. While the senior commanders still come from the ranks of the fighters, they are vastly outnumbered by non–warrior officers. This has created management problems in that the tail (support troops) has an increasing tendency to wag the dog (the warriors). While support troops are critical to the effective performance of modern armed forces, it's still the warriors that do the actual fighting. But in peacetime, the warrior generals are increasingly outnumbered by the camp follower generals, and this has led to less of a "warrior" mentality and more of a "camp follower" one. Naturally, in pitched battle, an army led by a warrior will trounce one led by a camp follower. But you need a real, live war to prove that, while in peacetime you can believe, or can convince the media and your superiors to embrace, whatever you want.

In the civilian sector, there has also been a noticeable growth in the proportion of "camp followers." Business enterprises have the advantage of being in combat all the time. When a firm starts to bleed red ink, and one of the problems turns out to be too many "camp followers," the excess people are promptly downsized and the company is made profitable again. Armed forces in peacetime have no balance sheet to keep them honest.

The great civilian manager must realize that in order to get projects completed, sufficient resources must be available and kept handy. An all-too-common reason for a project getting sidetracked, and failing, is senior people coming in and adding nonessential chores. Great Captains often get hit with this sort of thing, too, when cronies, or their king, intervenes with special requests. Members of a project team cannot be worried about activities or events that should be handled by others. Companies must be organized in a way so that support is given in the most effective way possible to project teams and those employees on the front lines. Managers who can organize things effectively will defeat their competition.

FLEXIBILITY AND ADAPTABILITY

The Great Captains realized that their plans and organizations were not set in stone. As a plan is executed, flaws may come to the attention of the person in charge. Great managers adapt their plans as they are executed. It is said that no battle plan survives contact with the enemy. This is true for the plans of business leaders as well. Great managers must be ready to think on their feet and be flexible to meet changing conditions and events that will affect their well-thought-out plans.

As Alexander and Genghis Khan went about conquering vast territories, they learned from the cultures they conquered. When they found a technique or a tool that would make them better at war or diplomacy, they adopted it. Caesar was noted, even in his own day, as a supreme opportunist. Caesar could turn just about any opportunity to his advantage. Even seeming disasters were turned into triumphs.

Caesar was eminently flexible and always on the lookout for new opportunities. Frederick the Great was another man of great flexibility and adaptability, taking seemingly hopeless situations and turning them to his advantage. He did it by being flexible in his negotiations and battlefield actions. Great managers also adopt the best practices when they find them. Too many business organizations will not change, and continue to practice business as they have in the past. Managers who wish to succeed must force their organizations to change and adopt new methods. Change is generally feared, but all too often the lack of change is worse. People tend to be more comfortable with what they know. But the problem here is a lack of curiosity and unwillingness to take the effort to investigate new methods and experiment with them. The Great Captains risked their lives to experiment and change, for a lost battle could be fatal even for the commander. Managers in a commercial operation risk far less than the Great Captains, and can gain almost as much by being the first to try something new.

TRAINING AND DISCIPLINE

One of the major mistake businesses and military commanders make is not investing enough in training. The Great Captains took a long time training and disciplining their troops. Genghis Khan, Frederick the Great, Schwarzkopf, Patton, Charlemagne, and Edward III were all great believers in training and discipline, and used those attributes to get ahead. Great managers also invest in the training of their employees. With new technologies and techniques entering the business arena every day, business leaders who neglect training risk falling behind their competition. Great managers realize that subordinates cannot be expected to master new techniques and technologies without proper training. If employees do not feel that their managers are investing in them by training them, they will leave to find companies that do invest in their employees.

Discipline is another area where managers have a more difficult time than generals. Discipline in the military is a matter of life and death. In a business it is a major contributor to success. But discipline is much harder to implement outside of the military. Soldiers are under the control of their officers all the time and, in most cases, can't just quit if they find the discipline too troublesome. Employees can quit and know that they have many ways to thwart attempts to enforce discipline. It takes more adroit leadership to introduce discipline into a business. But the payoffs are considerable for those who make the effort. One of the reasons government organizations are much less efficient than commercial ones is the relative lack of discipline compared to profit-making enterprises. Discipline takes competent leadership to enforce, and most government organizations do not attract the best managers. Moreover, one cannot just "order" discipline. One has to inspire and lead employees to operate in a disciplined and efficient manner. It's a challenge, but one with a big payoff.

MENTORS AND SELF-DEVELOPMENT

The Great Captains were all well educated. Most were brilliant by any measure. MacArthur in particular was regarded as the brightest officer in the army. All the Great Captains kept learning throughout their lives. During their earlier years, many of the Great Captains had mentors tutoring them in the ways of war. Staying ahead of their contemporaries in professional knowledge was a common trait of the Great Captains. All of the Great Captains attached themselves to exceptional men of their day, to learn the ropes, as it were. In turn, the Great Captains accepted younger men looking for a mentor. These protégés were useful as skilled subordinates. No Great Captain ever thought of doing it all by himself. They needed assistants, and knew that superior subordinates would make success come faster. By selecting up-and-coming young officers to join the Great Captain's inner circle, one could command intense performance. Frederick the Great was also able to delve into the arts, and composed music that is still appreciated two centuries later. Today, great managers find associates and superiors who can mentor them in the ways of business. Great business leaders, as well as Great Captains, realize that their education does not stop when they leave college or high school. Becoming a master of warfare, or a master of business, is a lifelong pursuit.

VISION

None of the Great Captains lacked a great vision. They all had a clear picture of the overall situation and what they could do to change things to their liking. Where does one get "the vision"? Often the great vision is nothing more than "get rich" or "get power" on a grand scale. But many Great Captains looked at their world and saw where they could change things in a major way. Business managers face the same opportunities, although less bloody ones.

All of our Great Captains set out purposely to implement their vision. They wanted to do great things and had a vision of how they would do them. Alexander wanted to conquer the world; Charlemagne wanted to redefine Europe; Patton wanted to outperform all the Great Captains of the past. Above all, the Great Captains wanted to make things happen, to bring about the kind of massive change that moved civilization forward.

Great managers must have great vision. They must see the possibilities that they can achieve. And then push themselves to achieve those visions. Truly great business leaders set for themselves great goals, then go after them. Great managers may not change the world, but they will most certainly change the commercial atmosphere around them.

DECISIVENESS

Being decisive and focused is a trait that is needed if a great manager wishes to win. Once any of the Great Captains had his mind fixed on a goal, he kept at it until the deed was done. Napoleon, for example, always knew what he wanted to achieve and how to get there. Too many managers today wander from one goal to the next. This was very unlike a Great Captain such as Gustavus, who used decisiveness to his advantage, both strategically and in the battles he fought. U. S. Grant could count decisiveness as his most effective trait. His predecessors tried leading the Union armies without decisiveness, and all of them failed. Grant succeeded.

Today's mangers often decide that the company is going to do one thing one day, and the next day they decide something else. The Great

Captains proved that once one has a goal in mind, the way to succeed was to keep working toward it. This is not to say that one doesn't make modifications, or make adjustments. It means that once they have decided what their goals are going to be great managers keep working at them no matter what disappointments come along, or what obstacles are thrown in their path. Frederick, for example, was successful because he would never quit once he was on his way to achieving a goal. Frederick would adapt as he went along, but he kept on going.

Decisiveness may be more a character trait than something that can really be learned. In any event, if you are not decisive, you can at least be aware of what kind of handicap you are operating under.

HIRING THE BEST AND KEEPING THEM

In some ways, this is a trite statement. Of course a manager wants to hire the best. Alexander, Genghis Khan, Gustavus, and MacArthur were particularly good at this, and they owed much of their success to a host of talented subordinates.

Many managers don't see the advantages of hiring the best. Too many managers see this policy as simply bringing in a lot of overpaid "troublesome people" and potential rivals. What it bought for the Great Captains was the ability to do a lot more with a lot less. For example, studies in the computer-programming field have consistently proven this. An excellent programmer will regularly outperform the average programmer by tenfold. This is not because good programmers can produce a greater volume of software, but that they tend to do it right the first time, fix it faster if they do make a mistake, and create code that is more easily maintained and modified. The Great Captains recognized how much more efficient good people are and surrounded themselves with the most able people they could find. In some cases these hotshots did prove troublesome, and there were times where a talented subordinate tried to replace his boss. The Great Captains were always up to the task of controlling their able associates. While Great Captains could attract skilled subordinates with the prospect of conquest and personal glory, modern managers have to offer a lot of money, a challenge, or the prospect of rapid advancement. But great managers know that the superior employee will return to them more productivity than the average employee, even after factoring in the additional compensation and other benefits.

The Great Captains also understood that after they hired the best troops, they also had to keep them around. The Great Captains did this by sharing the spoils of war, by handing out medals and honors, and by promoting the best soldiers as fast as possible. Great managers will find ways to share the profits with their employees, and they will find creative ways to honor and reward them.

INNOVATION AND USING TECHNOLOGY

It was common for many of the Great Captains to use innovation and technology to achieve their goals. Genghis Khan was a keen user of technology, despite being castigated as a crude barbarian. Frederick was another enthusiastic user of new technology, as was U. S. Grant. MacArthur rarely gets credit for being a great fan of technology, but indeed he was.

The Great Captains were always well versed in how to use the technology available to them. But many were not content with the status quo and were constantly looking for ways to improve things. If they themselves were not the innovators, they found someone else with a creative streak or advanced, for the time, technology. We tend to think that this use of new technology is a largely modern development, but even Alexander proved innovative and keen to make the most with technology that was available. Genghis Khan made it a policy to seek out new technology whenever a new area was conquered. Gustavus and Frederick both had an official policy of innovation exploiting new technology. There was more technology appearing in the seventeenth and eighteenth centuries, and these two Great Captains were quick to make the most of it.

Great managers will challenge the status quo, looking for new ways to do things. Business leaders should seek out innovators to help improve their business processes. Many of the changes the Great Captains put to work for them were based on new technology they had made a point of searching out and studying. Great managers of today need to be aware of technology and the possibilities that it can bring. The use of technology itself does not bring success. Artillery was around for a long time before Gustavus and Frederick began to use it more effectively on the battlefield. In order to get technology to work for the great managers, the great managers must understand its potential, or hire people who do.

Modern managers are inundated with new technology, often to the point of not knowing which of the many gadgets will actually do them any good. With all the new twentieth-century high tech comes new sales methods that seek to sell the sizzle when there is really no steak available. The Great Captains solved the problem of sorting out new technology by keenly observing how others used it. In a word, be wary of using any new technology first. It isn't innovative to be first, it is innovative to be the first one to make the new technology do something useful. "New technology" isn't what it used to be.

ALLIANCES

Alliances are as important in today's business world as they were to the Great Captains of the past. All the Great Captains used alliances to some extent, and used them successfully. The Great Captains knew that even enemies could be, at times, partners. And that neighbors were always useful, if only as neutrals.

Many goals in the business world can only be achieved with partners. In today's world there is no way that one company can do everything and stay in business. One's suppliers and vendors augment what one does in necessary ways. But leaders need to be careful in choosing their strategic partners, for these allies will determine overall strategy to some degree. Sometimes the Great Captains were forced to team up with someone they would rather avoid. But if they were careful not to get too cozy with their new partner, there would be benefits without the potential downside. The Great Captains would work with the undesirable ally as long as it made sense and there was benefit to them. Strategic partnerships should never be maintained unless there is perceived benefit to both parties. Great Captains were usually adept at making these alliances work for themselves even when the other party was not getting much benefit. Effective alliances require some adroit diplomacy and keen deal making. Caesar, Gustavus, and Napoleon were masters at this kind of alliance building, and how they did it still provides lessons to modern managers.

POWER OF PERSONALITY

The Great Captains all had powerful personalities. This does not mean that they were all over-the-top egomaniacs. Some were. What it does mean is that they all had core principles and values that ran deep in their personalities. And they were not afraid to act out their values and principles. They lived how they wanted to live and not as others would have them. Even the quiet and unassuming U. S. Grant had a strong personality. These traits can be developed, but it takes concentration and effort. Patton decided what type of personality he wanted and made it so. MacArthur was famous, and infamous, for his "acting out." But he made it work, even though many still argue over how far he went while doing it. Norman Schwarzkopf had a passion for what he believed in which kept him going. Like MacArthur, he took hits in the media for being "too enthusiastic." You can't be "too enthusiastic" if you have something worth doing and are on your way to getting it done.

Good managers can determine the values and characteristics they wish to have and then work on them daily to transform themselves into great managers. But you must be able to develop a personality that can project these values. Some managers can do it quietly, others go for the more outspoken approach. Doesn't matter which way you go, as long as you pull it off. You can learn many effective techniques from the Great Captains.

Most Great Captains had personalities that any politician would be eager to possess. These personalities were usually based on a powerful speaking ability. Being persuasive in front of an audience is always a key leadership skill, and the Great Captains all had it to one degree or another. Most also possessed considerable personal charm. The Great Captains could go one on one with a general or soldier and leave a most favorable impression. Most Great Captains also had the ability to put on an impressive show whenever they appeared. Even if they were not physically striking (as most were), they would dress and act as someone worth following anywhere.

Not surprisingly, the same personality traits the Great Captains cultivated have proven equally useful for contemporary executives. Making a splash when you arrive anywhere is still considered advantageous, and not just for celebrities. Indeed, exceptionally successful business executives move about like they are celebrities, and some of them, for all practical purposes, are. There are now consultants who will tutor managers on how to give a speech effectively or how to act in front of a camera. Julius Caesar would have understood all this.

LOGISTICS AND SPEED

While most of the Great Captains' skills are directly transferable to the civilian manager's world, two are not. Or at least not without a bit of explanation and modification.

Logistics is the process of keeping the troops supplied. Getting ammunition, fuel, food, and other items to the soldiers, at all times and despite all problems, is what separates the really professional commanders from the amateurs. Speed is how quickly a commander can move his troops about and have them execute maneuvers (attack, defend, dig in) in a combat zone. All Great Captains possess these two skills, often in great abundance.

In the civilian sector, logistics occupies a more prosaic role, or at least it has until recently. Speed has always been rather more important, but has become even more essential today.

Logistics is now a hot topic for managers. "Just in time" inventory and getting all manner of "things" delivered quickly have become significant commercial advantages. Everything moves more quickly in the late twentieth century. The Great Captains solved their logistics problems using logic, systematic planning, and a lot of original thinking. That approach can still work today. Look at the development of companies like FedEx and UPS to see how Great Captains of industry have solved modern logistical problems and turned them to their advantage. Even a much maligned organization like the U. S. Postal Service is, despite all the gibes, the most effective postal service in the world and carries 40 percent of all the planet's mail. And does it cheaper than anyone else. Within many large companies, new thinking about logistics has improved operations and profits. Logistics is no longer mundane.

Speed has always been an advantage in military affairs. Speed in everything, from planning to getting troops trained to the obvious need for speed in combat. What makes the experience of the Great Captains useful is that in almost all cases they were using speed with large, complex organizations. And doing so under great stress. Throughout the twentieth century, speed has loomed larger as a factor in business success. The Japanese in particular showed how speed in developing new products, and tooling up production, was an enormous advantage that all their competitors must now match. Thus the experiences of the Great Captains in this area become more pertinent. The Great Captains obtained the speed they needed by using just about all of their skills.

Speed is not something one can just pull off the shelf. To obtain speed in war or commercial operations, one must organize for it, train for it, select like-minded subordinates for it, plan for it, and execute with vigor. Speedy execution is so valuable partly because so few generals, or managers, can pull it off.

OTHER SKILLS

Great Captains had a large inventory of skills and talents upon which to draw. In addition to the commonly used ones discussed above, there were a number that were unique to only a few of our Great Captains.

Both Norman Schwarzkopf and Alexander had an awareness of other cultures, and the ability to work with them, that served them well. In a world where international trade and multinational corporations are increasingly important, cultural awareness is an ever more important trait. Actually, many successful military leaders in this century used cultural awareness to their advantage. And many more business managers are profitably following that example. It's not so difficult to develop cultural awareness. It helps a lot to speak foreign languages, but a manager can achieve a useful degree of cultural awareness simply by studying other cultures and dealing with them respectfully.

Frederick and U. S. Grant both made much of learning from their mistakes. All Great Captains do this to some degree, but these two generals capitalized on their errors and disasters to build new habits and techniques. This was a personality thing for them, but anyone can use their technique. Basically, they saw mistakes not as unmitigated disasters, not something to be gotten over and forgotten, but as opportunities to learn and change their ways. It worked. Still does. One doesn't often hear of the leisure-time activities of the Great Captains, but they all had things they liked to do when off duty. Two Great Captains in general, Frederick and Schwarzkopf, used their hobbies to enhance their primary (war-making) skills. Frederick found the company of intellectuals and musicians, as well as composing and performing music himself, to be relaxing and a good way to recharge his batteries. General Schwarzkopf has a more prosaic list of pastimes, but they perform the same function as Frederick's. Schwarzkopf's hobbies are rather more common with modern military men, what with longer stretches of peacetime tedium between the wars. As the ancient advice goes, all work and no play makes for a dull person. It's a rule that is ignored at one's peril.

A large proportion of the Great Captains were well versed in economic matters. This is understandable, as many were heads of state as well as warlords. But not all national leaders paid much attention to financial and economic matters. So in this respect, the Great Captains who did were again at the head of the pack. Edward III used some innovative financing to maintain his long war with France. Gustavus and Caesar had to be equally clever to keep their own wars going. Charlemagne was exceptional in the way he used economic reforms to strengthen his empire. In fact, all the Great Captains used clever financial techniques to one degree or another. They understood the importance of finance and followed the money.

The Great Captains used a number of innovative techniques to cope with the tremendous fiscal burdens of combat. Warfare has always been expensive. Just as nations at war in this century regularly applied over two-thirds of their annual government revenues to military matters, so did kingdoms in the past. But even that great a fraction of national income was not enough. The Great Captains were not wanting when it came to novel ideas for solving fiscal problems. Alexander decided to absorb his largest (and better-financed) competitor, the Persian Empire. Edward III did a similar deal, using plunder from campaigning in France to maintain his armies. Edward also arranged to discharge unneeded troops in France and didn't mind terribly much when many of these unemployed soldiers formed themselves into mercenary companies and went right back to pillaging France.

Napoleon also plundered France to finance his wars, but he did so as emperor of France, and the head of the first modern police state. No wonder Hitler admired Napoleon so much. Napoleon also used diplomacy and threats to extort vast sums from his European allies. Genghis Khan also employed extortion on a large scale, but he also instituted efficient governments in his conquered territories to keep the loot coming on an organized basis. That said, it is also obvious that the Great Captains often put themselves beyond any laws when they operated these massive extortion schemes. Not every technique of the Great Captains is worthy of emulation.

All Great Captains had, to varying degrees, "situational awareness." This is the ability to size up new situations promptly. To a large degree, one is either born with this one, or not. But if one has it, one should develop it further and use it all one can. It's not for nothing that situational awareness is called the "Ace Factor"; the trait that separates average fighter pilots from those who sweep the skies of the enemy.

Great Captains were good at sizing up their opponents. Part of this was situational awareness, but more often it was the ability to collect information on the enemy and sort it out. There are many ways one can do this. The important thing is just to do it.

Great Captains were solution-oriented. They didn't dawdle when they encountered a problem, but promptly got to work developing a solution. Granted, Great Captains were often faced with death if they didn't solve many of their problems, but managers can learn from their experience without the "do or die" incentive.

Great Captains were, above all, original thinkers who had the courage and will to risk all by implementing their plans. Just like many very successful businessmen. Except that the Great Captains did it under fire and risked their lives as well as their net worth.

While the Great Captains went about their business of warfare at great personal risk, most of their lives were spent solving the same business problems managers still struggle with. War, then and now, consists of a little fighting and a whole lot of managing. The former is usually not possible without the latter, although ultimately one has to fight. But the warrior with the best management skills generally wins.

This is true on and off the battlefield.

Keep it in mind.

FURTHER READING

THE GREAT CAPTAINS discussed in this work have had thousands of books written about them. Some, like Napoleon, are the subject of thousands of works, and more appear each year. Others, like Charlemagne, have been much less written about. In addition, many of the Great Captains were themselves authors, and most of their works are still in print. We used hundreds of these books to prepare this volume. It's difficult to determine which one of the available sources would be best for your particular needs. Instead, we direct you to World Wide Web booksellers who have search engines available to find books on the Great Captains and other subjects that you might wish to find more information on. One of the best of these sites is Amazon Books, found at www.amazon.com. There are others, as well as large libraries containing out-of-print works.

The more recent works tend to incorporate the latest research on a particular subject, although many of the older works still stand up well by themselves.

Good hunting.

INDEX